THE
EARLY
YEARS

THE
EARLY
YEARS

The Lyrics of
Tom Waits

{1971–1982}

ecco
An Imprint of HarperCollinsPublishers

HarperCollins books may be purchased for educational, business, or sales
promotional use. For information, please write: Special Markets Department,
HarperCollins Publishers, 10 East 53rd Street, New York, NY 10022.

An extension of this copyright page appears opposite.

FIRST EDITION

Designed by Nicola Ferguson

Library of Congress Cataloging-in-Publication Data is available upon request.

ISBN: 978-0-06-145800-2
ISBN-10: 0-06-145800-7

07 08 09 10 11   ID/RRD   10 9 8 7 6 5 4 3 2 1

Contents

CLOSING
TIME

Ol' 55

Well my time went so quickly,
I went lickety-splickly out to my old '55
As I drove away slowly, feeling so holy,
God knows, I was feeling alive.

Now the sun's coming up,
I'm riding with Lady Luck,
freeway cars and trucks,
Stars beginning to fade,
and I lead the parade

Just a-wishing I'd stayed a little longer,
Oh, Lord, let me tell you
that the feeling's getting stronger.

And it's six in the morning,
gave me no warning; I had to be on my way.
Well there's trucks all a-passing me,
and the lights are all flashing,
I'm on my way home from your place.

And now the sun's coming up,
I'm riding with Lady Luck,
freeway cars and trucks,
Stars beginning to fade,
and I lead the parade

Just a-wishing I'd stayed a little longer,
Oh, Lord, let me tell you
that the feeling's getting stronger.

And my time went so quickly,
I went lickety-splickly out to my old '55
As I pulled away slowly, feeling so holy,
God knows, I was feeling alive.

Now the sun's coming up,
I'm riding with Lady Luck,
Freeway cars and trucks,
freeway cars and trucks,
freeway cars and trucks . . .

I Hope That I Don't Fall
in Love with You

Well I hope that I don't fall in love with you
'Cause falling in love just makes me blue,
Well the music plays and you display
your heart for me to see,
I had a beer and now I hear you
calling out for me
And I hope that I don't fall in love with you.

Well the room is crowded, people everywhere
And I wonder, should I offer you a chair?
Well if you sit down with this old clown,
take that frown and break it,
Before the evening's gone away,
I think that we could make it,
And I hope that I don't fall in love with you.

Well the night does funny things inside a man
These old tom-cat feelings you don't understand,
Well I turn around to look at you,
you light a cigarette,
I wish I had the guts to bum one,
but we've never met,
And I hope that I don't fall in love with you.

I can see that you are lonesome just like me,
and it being late, you'd like some some company,
Well I turn around to look at you,
and you look back at me,
The guy you're with has up and split,
the chair next to you's free,
And I hope that you don't fall in love with me.

Now it's closing time, the music's fading out
Last call for drinks, I'll have another stout.
Well I turn around to look at you,
you're nowhere to be found,
I search the place for your lost face,
guess I'll have another round
And I think that I just fell in love with you.

Virginia Avenue

Well, I'm walking on down Virginia Avenue
Trying to find somebody to tell my troubles to.
Harold's club is closing,

and everybody's going on home:
What's a poor boy to do?

I'll just get on back into my short,
make it back to the fort
Sleep off all the crazy lizards inside of my brain.
There's got to be some place
that's better than this
This life I'm leading's driving me insane

And let me tell you I'm dreaming . . .

Let me tell you that
I'm dreaming to the twilight,
this town has got me down.
I've seen all the highlights,
I've been walking all around
I won't make a fuss, I'll take a Greyhound bus,
carry me away from here:
Tell me, what have I got to lose?

'Cause I'm walking on down Columbus Avenue
The bars are all closing,
'cause it's quarter to two
Every town I go to is like a lock without a key
Those I leave behind are catching up on me,
Let me tell you they're catching up on me,

they're catching up on me
Catching up on me, catching up on me,
catching up on me.

Old Shoes (And Picture Postcards)

I'm singing this song, it's time it was sung
I've been putting it off for a while,
But it's harder by now, 'cause the truth is so clear
That I cry when I'm seeing you smile.
So goodbye, so long, the road calls me dear
And your tears cannot bind me anymore,
And farewell to the girl with the sun in her eyes
Can I kiss you, and then I'll be gone.

Every time that I tried to tell
that we'd lost the magic we had at the start,
I would weep my heart when I looked in your eyes
And I searched once again for the spark.
So goodbye, so long, the road calls me dear
And your tears cannot bind me anymore,
And farewell to the girl with the sun in her eyes
Can I kiss you, and then I'll be gone.

I can see by your eyes, it's time now to go
So I'll leave you to cry in the rain,
Though I held in my hand, the key to all joy
Honey my heart was not born to be tamed.
So goodbye, so long, the road calls me dear
And your tears cannot bind me anymore,
And farewell to the girl with the sun in her eyes
Can I kiss you, and then I'll be gone.

So goodbye, so long, the road calls me dear
And your tears cannot bind me anymore,
And farewell to the girl with the sun in her eyes
Can I kiss you, and then I'll be gone,
Can I kiss you, and then I'll be gone,
can I kiss you, and then I'll be gone.

Midnight Lullaby

Sing a song of sixpence, pocket full of rye
Hush-a bye my baby, no need to be crying.
You can burn the midnight oil with me
as long as you will
Stare out at the moon
upon the windowsill, and dream . . .

Sing a song of sixpence, pocket full of rye
Hush-a bye my baby, no need to be crying.
There's dew drops on the window sill,
gumdrops in your head
Slipping into dream land,
you're nodding your head, so dream . . .

Dream of West Virginia, or of the British Isles
'Cause when you are dreaming,
you see for miles and miles.
When you are much older, remember when we sat
At midnight on the windowsill,
and had this little chat
And dream, come on and dream,
come on and dream, and dream, and dream . . .

Martha

Operator, number, please:
it's been so many years
Will she remember my old voice
while I fight the tears?
Hello, hello there, is this Martha?
this is old Tom Frost,
And I am calling long distance,
don't worry 'bout the cost.
'Cause it's been forty years or more,
now Martha please recall,
Meet me out for coffee,
where we'll talk about it all.

And those were the days of roses,
poetry and prose and Martha
all I had was you and all you had was me.
There was no tomorrows,
we'd packed away our sorrows
And we saved them for a rainy day.

And I feel so much older now,
and you're much older too,
How's your husband?
and how's the kids?
you know that I got married too?
Lucky that you found someone
to make you feel secure,
'Cause we were all so young and foolish,
now we are mature.

And those were the days of roses,
poetry and prose and Martha

all I had was you and all you had was me.
There was no tomorrows,
we'd packed away our sorrows
And we saved them for a rainy day.

And I was always so impulsive,
I guess that I still am,
And all that really mattered then
was that I was a man.
I guess that our being together
was never meant to be.
And Martha, Martha,
I love you can't you see?

And those were the days of roses,
poetry and prose and Martha
all I had was you and all you had was me.
There was no tomorrows,
we'd packed away our sorrows
And we saved them for a rainy day.

And I remember quiet evenings
trembling close to you . . .

Rosie

Well I'm sitting on a windowsill, blowing my horn
Nobody's up except the moon and me,
And a lazy old tomcat on a midnight spree
All that you left me was a melody.
Rosie, why do you evade? Rosie,
how can I persuade? Rosie . . .

And the moon's all up, full and big,
apricot tips in an indigo sky,
And I've been loving you, Rosie,
since the day I was born
And I'll love you, Rosie 'til the day I die.
Rosie, why do you evade? Rosie,
how can I persuade? Rosie . . .

Rosie, why do you evade? Rosie,
how can I persuade? Rosie . . .

And I'm sitting on a windowsill, blowing my horn
Nobody's up except the moon and me,
And a lazy old tomcat on a midnight spree
All that you left me was a melody.
Rosie, why do you evade?
Rosie, how can I persuade? Rosie . . .

Lonely

Lonely, lonely, lonely, lonely eyes,
lonely face, lonely lonely in your place.
Lonely, lonely, lonely eyes, lonely face,
lonely lonely in your place.

I thought that I knew all that there was to,
lonely, lonely, lonely . . .

Melanie Jane, won't feel the pain.
Lonely, lonely, lonely eyes, lonely eyes,
lonely lonely in your place.

And I thought that I knew all that there was to
Lonely, lonely, lonely eyes, lonely eyes,
lonely lonely in your place, and
I still love you, I still love you,
lonely, lonely . . .

Ice Cream Man

I'll be clickin' by your house about two forty-five
Sidewalk sundae strawberry surprise,
I got a cherry popsicle right on time
A big stick, mamma, that'll blow your mind

'Cause I'm the ice cream man,
I'm a one-man band (yeah)
I'm the ice cream man, honey,
I'll be good to you.

Baby, missed me in the alley, baby, don't you fret
Come back around and don't forget,
When you're tired and you're hungry
and you want something cool,
Got something better than a swimming pool

'Cause I'm the ice cream man,
I'm a one-man band
I'm the ice cream man, honey,
I'll be good to you.
'Cause I'm the ice cream man,
I'm a one-man band
I'm the ice cream man, honey,
I'll be good to you.

See me coming, you ain't got no change
Don't worry baby, it can be arranged:
Show me you can smile, baby just for me
Fix you with a drumstick, I'll do it for free

'Cause I'm the ice cream man, I'm a one-man band
I'm the ice cream man, honey, I'll be good to you.

Be good to you, be good to you,
Good to you yeah, good to you yeah,
good to you yeah, good to you yeah,
Good to you yeah, good to you,
I'll be good to you, I'll be good to you . . .

Little Trip to Heaven
(On the Wings of your Love)

Lazy trip to heaven on the wings of your love
Banana moon is shining in the sky,
Feel like I'm in heaven when you're with me
Know that I'm in heaven when you smile,
Though we're stuck here on the ground,
I got something that I've found
And it's you.

And I don't have to take no trip to outer space
All I have to do is look at your face,
And before I know it, I'm in orbit around you
Thanking my lucky stars that I've found you,
When I see your constellation,
honey, you're my inspiration,
and it's you.

You're my north star when I'm lost and feeling blue,
The sun is breaking through the clouds
don't you, don't you know it's true?
Honey, all the other stars seem dim around you
Thanking my lucky stars that I've found you,
When I see your smiling face, honey,
I know nothing ever going to take your place,
and it's you.

And it's you, and it's you,
and it's you, and it's you, and it's you
And it's you, and it's you, shoo-be-doo, ba-da-da.

Grapefruit Moon

Grapefruit moon, one star shining,
shining down on me.
Heard that tune, and now I'm pining,
honey, can't you see?
'Cause every time I hear that melody,
well, something breaks inside,
And the grapefruit moon, one star shining,
can't turn back the tide.

Never had no destination, could not get across.
You became my inspiration, oh but what a cost.
'Cause every time I hear that melody,
well, something breaks inside,
And the grapefruit moon, one star shining,
is more than I can hide.

Now I'm smoking cigarettes
and I strive for purity,
And I slip just like the stars into obscurity.
'Cause every time I hear that melody,
well, puts me up a tree,
And the grapefruit moon, one star shining,
is all that I can see.

THE HEART OF SATURDAY NIGHT

New Coat Of Paint

Let's put a new coat of paint on this lonesome old town
Set 'em up, we'll be knockin' 'em down.
You wear a dress, baby, and I'll wear a tie.
We'll laugh at that old bloodshot moon in that burgundy sky

All your scribbled lovedreams, are lost or thrown away,
Here amidst the shuffle of an overflowing day
Our love needs a transfusion so let's shoot it full of wine
Fishin' for a good time starts with throwin'in your line.

San Diego Serenade

I never saw the morning 'til I stayed up all night
I never saw the sunshine 'til you turned out the light
I never saw my hometown until I stayed away too long
I never heard the melody, until I needed a song.

I never saw the white line, 'til I was leaving you behind
I never knew I needed you 'til I was caught up in a bind
I never spoke 'I love you' 'til I cursed you in vain,
I never felt my heartstrings until I nearly went insane.

I never saw the east coast 'til I move to the west
I never saw the moonlight until it shone off your breast
I never saw your heart 'til someone tried to steal,
tried to steal it away
I never saw your tears until they rolled down your face.

Semi Suite

Well you hate those diesels rollin'
And those Friday nights out bowlin'
When he's off for a twelve hour lay over night

You wish you had a dollar
For every time he hollered
That he's leavin'
And he's never comin' back

But the curtain-laced billow
And his hands on your pillow
And his trousers are hangin' on the chair

You're lyin' through your pain, babe
But you're gonna tell him he's your man
And you ain't got the courage to leave

He tells you that you're on his mind
You're the only one he's ever gonna find
It's kind-a special, understands his complicated soul . . .

But the only place a man can breathe
And collect his thoughts is
Midnight and flyin' away on the road.

But you've packed and unpacked
So many times you've lost track
And the steam heat is drippin' off the walls

But when you hear his engines
You're lookin' through the window in the kitchen and you know

You're always gonna be there when he calls
'Cause he's a truck drivin' man
Stoppin' when he can
He's a truck drivin' man
Stoppin' when he can

Shiver Me Timbers

I'm leavin' my fam'ly
Leavin' all my friends
My body's at home
But my heart's in the wind
Where the clouds are like headlines
On a new front page sky
My tears are salt water
And the moon's full and high

And I know Martin Eden's
Gonna be proud of me
And many before me
Who've been called by the sea
To be up in the crow's nest
Singin' my say
Shiver me Timbers
'Cause I'm a-sailin' away

And the fog's liftin'
And the sand's shiftin'
I'm driftin' on out
Ol' Captain Ahab
He ain't got nothin' on me, now.
So swallow me, don't follow me
I'm trav'lin' alone
Blue water's my daughter
'n I'm gonna skip like a stone

So please call my missus
Gotta tell her not to cry
'Cause my goodbye is written
By the moon in the sky

Hey and nobody knows me
I can't fathom my stayin'
Shiver me timbers
'Cause I'm a-sailin' away

And the fog's liftin'
And the sand's shiftin'
I'm driftin' on out
Ol' Captain Ahab
He ain't got nothin' on me
So come and swallow me, follow me
I'm trav'lin' alone
Blue water's my daughter
'n I'm gonna skip like a stone

And I'm leavin' my family
Leavin' all my friends
My body's at home
But my heart's in the wind
Where the clouds are like headlines
Upon a new front page sky
And shiver me timbers
'Cause I'm a-sailin' away

Diamonds on my Windshield

Diamonds on my windshield
Tears from heaven
Pulling into town on the Interstate
Pulling a steel train in the rain
The wind bites my cheek through the wing
Fast flying, freeway driving
Always makes me sing

There's a Duster tryin' to change my tune
Pulling up fast on the right
Rolling restlessly, twenty-four hour moon

Wisconsin hiker with a cue-ball head
Wishing he was home in a Wiscosin bed
fifteen feet of snow in the East
Colder then a welldigger's ass

Oceanside it ends the ride, San Clemente coming up
Sunday desperadoes slip by, gas station closed,
cruise with a dry back
Orange drive-in the neon billin'
Theatre's fillin' to the brim
Slave girls and a hot spurn bucket full of sin

Metropolitan area with interchange and connections
Fly-by-nights from Riverside
Black and white plates, out of state,
running a little bit late

Sailors jockey for the fast lane
101 don't miss it

Rolling hills and concrete fields
The broken line's on your mind

Eights go east and the fives go north
The merging nexus back and forth
You see your sign, cross the line,
signalling with a blink

The radio's gone off the air
Gives you time to think
You ease it out and you creep across
Intersection light goes out
You hear the rumble
As you fumble for a cigarette
Blazing through this midnight jungle
Remember someone that you met
One more block; the engine talks
And whispers 'home at last'
It whispers, whispers, whispers
'home at last,' home at last

(Looking For) The Heart
of Saturday Night

Well you gassed her up
Behind the wheel
With your arm around your sweet one
In your Oldsmobile
Barrelin' down the boulevard
You're looking for the heart of Saturday night

And you got paid on Friday
And your pockets are jinglin'
And you see the lights
You get all tinglin' cause you're cruisin' with a 6
And you're looking for the heart of Saturday night

Then you comb your hair
Shave your face
Tryin' to wipe out ev'ry trace
All the other days
In the week you know that this'll be the Saturday
You're reachin' your peak

Stoppin' on the red
You're goin' on the green
'Cause tonight'll be like nothin'
You've ever seen
And you're barrelin' down the boulevard
Lookin' for the heart of Saturday night

Tell me is the crack of the poolballs, neon buzzin'?
Telephone's ringin'; it's your second cousin
Is it the barmaid that's smilin' from the corner of her eye?
Magic of the melancholy tear in your eye.

Makes it kind of quiver down in the core
'Cause you're dreamin' of them Saturdays that came before
And now you're stumblin'
You're stumblin' onto the heart of Saturday night

Well you gassed her up
And you're behind the wheel
With your arm around your sweet one
In your Oldsmobile
Barrellin' down the boulevard,
You're lookin' for the heart of Saturday night

Is the crack of the poolballs, neon buzzin'?
Telephone's ringin'; it's your second cousin
And the barmaid is smilin' from the corner of her eye
Magic of the melancholy tear in your eye.

Makes it kind of special down in the core
And you're dreamin' of them Saturdays that came before
It's found you stumblin'
Stumblin' onto the heart of Saturday night
And you're stumblin'
Stumblin' onto the heart of Saturday night

Fumblin' With the Blues

Friday left me fumblin' with the blues
And it's hard to win when you always lose
Because the nightspots spend your spirit
Beat your head against the wall
Two dead ends and you've still got to choose

You know the bartenders
They all know my name
And they catch me when I'm pulling up lame
And I'm a pool-shooting-shimmy-shyster shaking my head
When I should be living clean instead

You know the ladies I've been seeing off and on
Well they spend your love and then they're gone
You can't be lovin' someone who is savage and cruel
Take your love and then they leave on out of town
No they do

Well now fallin' in love is such a breeze
But its standin' up that's so hard for me
I wanna squeeze you but I'm scared to death I'd break your back
You know your perfume
Well it won't let me be

You know the bartenders all know my name
And they catch me when I'm pulling up lame
And I'm a pool-shooting-shimmy-shyster shaking my head
When I should be living clean instead

Come on baby
Let your love light shine
Gotta bury me inside of your fire

Because your eyes are 'nough to blind me
You're like a-looking at the sun
You gotta whisper tell me I'm the one
Come on and whisper tell me I'm the one
Gotta whisper tell me I'm the one
Come on and whisper tell me I'm the one

Please Call Me, Baby

The evening fell just like a star
Left a trail behind
You spit as you slammed out the door
If this is love we're crazy
As we fight like cats and dogs
But I just know there's got to be more

So please call me, baby
Wherever you are
It's too cold to be out walking in the streets
We do crazy things when we're wounded
Everyone's a bit insane
I don't want you catching your death of cold
Out walking in the rain

I admit that I ain't no angel
I admit that I ain't no saint
I'm selfish and I'm cruel and I'm blind
If I exorcise my devils
Well my angels may leave too
When they leave they're so hard to find

[chorus]

We're always at each other's throats
It drives me up the wall
Most of the time I'm just blowing off steam
And I wish to God you'd leave me
And I wish to God you'd stay
Life's so different than it is in your dreams

[chorus]

Depot, Depot

Depot, depot, what am I doing here?
Depot, depot, what am I doing here?
I ain't coming, I ain't going
My confusion is showing
Outside the midnight wind is blowing Sixth Avenue
I'm gonna paint myself blue
At the depot

I watch the taxis pull up and idle
I can't claim title to a single memory
He offered me a key
'Cause opportunity don't knock
He has no tongue and she cannot talk
You're gonna shuffle when you walk
At the depot

This peeping-Tom needs a peephole
And an uptempo song
To move me along
When I find this depot baby
I'm on a roll just like a pool ball baby
I'm gonna be there at the roll call maybe
At the depot

Outside the midnight wind is blowing Sixth Avenue
Oh, tell me what a poor boy to do
At the depot
I'm on a roll just like a pool ball baby
I'm gonna be there at the roll call maybe
At the depot
The depot

Drunk on the Moon

Tight-slacked clad girls on the graveyard shift
'Neath the cement stroll
Catch the midnight drift
Cigar chewing charlie
In that newspaper nest
grifting hot horse tips
On who's running the best

And I'm blinded by the neon
Don't try and change my tune
'Cause I thought I heard a saxophone
I'm drunk on the moon

And the moon's a silver slipper
It's pouring champagne stars
Broadway's like a serpent
Pulling shiny top-down cars
Laramer is teeming
With that undulating beat
And some Bonneville is screaming
It's way wilder down the street

[chorus]

Hearts flutter and race
The moon's on the wane
Tarts mutter their dream hopes
The night will ordain
Come schemers and dancers
Cherry delight
As a Cleveland-bound Greyhound

And it cuts throught the night
And I've hawked all my yesterdays
Don't try and change my tune
'Cause I thought I heard a saxophone
I'm drunk on the moon

The Ghosts of Saturday Night
(After Hours at Napoleone's Pizza House)

A cab combs the snake,
Tryin' to rake in that last night's fare,
And a solitary sailor
Who spends the facts of his life
like small change on strangers . . .

Paws his inside P-coat pocket
for a welcome twenty-five cents,
And the last bent butt from a package of Kents,
As he dreams of a waitress with Maxwell House eyes
And marmalade thighs with scrambled yellow hair.

Her rhinestone-studded moniker says, "Irene"
As she wipes the wisps of dishwater blonde from her eyes

And the Texaco beacon burns on,
The steel-belted attendant with a 'Ring and Valve Special' . . .
Cryin' "Fill'er up and check that oil"
"You know it could be a distributor and it could be a coil."

The early mornin' final edition's on the stands,
And that town cryer's cryin' there with nickels in his hands.
Pigs in a blanket sixty-nine cents,
Eggs—roll 'em over and a package of Kents,
Adam and Eve on a log, you can sink 'em damn straight,
Hash browns, hash browns, you know I can't be late.

And the early dawn cracks out a carpet of diamond
Across a cash crop car lot
filled with twilight Coupe Devilles,
Leaving the town in a-keeping
Of the one who is sweeping
Up the ghost of Saturday night . . .

NIGHTHAWKS
AT THE
DINER

Emotional Weather Report

late night and early morning low clouds
with a chance of fog
chance of showers into the afternoon
with variable high cloudiness
and gusty winds, gusty winds
at times around the corner of
Sunset and Alvorado
things are tough all over
when the thunder storms start
increasing over the southeast
and south central portions
of my apartment, I get upset
and a line of thunderstorms was
developing in the early morning
ahead of a slow moving coldfront
cold blooded
with tornado watches issued shortly
before noon Sunday, for the areas
including, the western region
of my mental health
and the northern portions of my
ability to deal rationally with my
disconcerted precarious emotional
situation, it's cold out there
colder than a ticket taker's smile
at the Ivar Theatre, on a Saturday night
flash flood watches covered the
southern portion of my disposition
there was no severe weather well
into the afternoon, except for a lone gust of
wind in the bedroom
in a high pressure zone, covering the eastern

portion of a small suburban community
with a 103 and millibar high pressure zone
and a weak pressure ridge extending from
my eyes down to my cheeks cause since
you left me baby
and put the vice grips on my mental health
well the extended outlook for an
indefinite period of time until you
come back to me baby is high tonight
low tomorrow, and precipitation is
expected

On a Foggy Night

on a foggy night, an abandoned road
in a twilight mirror mirage
with no indication of a service station
or an all night garage, I was misinformed
I was misdirected cause the interchange
never intersected leaving me marooned
beneath a bloodshot moon
all upon a foggy night, on a foggy night
an abandoned road, in a blurred brocade
collage, is that a road motel?
I can't really tell, is that what you
might call some kind of a vacancy lodge
cause there's no consolation, what
kind of situation to be aimlessly skewed
amidst a powder blue?
no tell tail light clue
spun like the spell you spin
this precarious pandemonium
I'm stranded, all upon a foggy night
all upon a foggy night
on a foggy night

Eggs & Sausage
(In a Cadillac With Susan Michelson)

nighthawks at the diner
of Emma's 49er, there's a rendezvous
of strangers around the coffee urn tonight
all the gypsy hacks, the insomniacs
now the paper's been read
now the waitress said

eggs and sausage and a side of toast
coffee and a roll, hash browns over easy
chile in a bowl with burgers and fries
what kind of pie?

In a graveyard charade, a late shift masquerade
2 for a quarter, dime for a dance
with Woolworth rhinestone diamond
earrings, and a sideway's glance
and now the register rings
and now the waitress sings

[chorus]

the classified section offered no direction
it's a cold caffeine in a nicotine cloud
now the touch of your fingers
lingers burning in my memory
I've been 86ed from your scheme
I'm in a melodramatic nocturnal scene
I'm a refugee from a disconcerted affair
as the lead pipe morning falls
and the waitress calls

[chorus]

Better Off Without a Wife

all my friends are married
every Tom and Dick and Harry
you must be strong
to go it alone
here's to the bachelors
and the bowery bums
and those who feel that they're the ones
who are better off without a wife

I like to sleep until the crack of noon
midnight howlin' at the moon
goin' out when I wanto, comin' home when I please
I don't have to ask permission
if I want to go out fishing
and I never have to ask for the keys

never been no Valentino
had a girl who lived in Reno
left me for a trumpet player
didn't get me down
he was wanted for assault
though he said it weren't his fault
well the coppers rode him right
out of town

[chorus]

selfish about my privacy
as long as I can be with me
we get along so well I can't believe
I love to chew the fat with folks
and listen to all your dirty jokes

I'm so thankful for these friends
I do receive

[chorus]

Nighthawk Postcards (From Easy Street)

there's a blur drizzle down the plateglass
as a neon swizzle stick stirrin' up the sultry night air
and a yellow biscuit of a buttery cue ball moon
rollin' maverick across an obsidian sky
as the busses go groanin' and wheezin',
down on the corner I'm freezin';
on a restless boulevard at a midnight road
I'm across town from EASY STREET
with the tight knots of moviegoers and out of towners
on the stroll
and the buildings towering high above
lit like dominoes or black dice
all the used car salesmen dressed up in
Purina Checkerboard slacks
and Foster Grant wrap-around,
pacing in front of EARL SCHLEIB
$39.95 merchandise
like barkers at a shootin' gallery
they throw out kind of a Texas Guinan routine
"Hello sucker, we like your money
just as well as anybody else's here"
or they give you the P.T. Barnum bit
"There's a sucker born every minute
you just happened to be comin' along at the right time"
come over here now
you know . . . all the harlequin sailors are on the stroll
in a search of "LIKE NEW," "NEW PAINT,"
decent factory air and AM-FM dreams
and the piss yellow gypsy cabs
stacked up in the taxi zones waitin' like
pinball machines
to be ticking off a joy ride to a magical place

waitin' in line like "truckers welcome" diners
with dirt lots full of
Peterbilts, Kenworths, Jimmy's and the like, and
they're hiballin' with bankrupt brakes, over driven
under paid, over fed, a day late and a dollar short
but Christ I got my lips around a bottle and
my foot on the throttle and I'm standin' on the corner
standin' on the corner like a "just in town"
jasper, on a street corner with a gasper lookin'
for some kind of Cheshire billboard grin
stroking a goateed chin, and using parking meters
as walking sticks on the inebriated stroll
with my eyelids propped open at half mast
but you know . . . over at Chubb's Pool Hall and Snooker
it was a nickle after two, yea it was a nickle after two
and in the cobalt steel blue dream smoke, it
was the radio that groaned out the hit parade
and the chalk squeaked, the floorboards creaked
and an Olympia sign winked through a torn yellow
shade, old Jack Chance himself leanin' up against
a Wurlitzer and eyeballin' out a 5 ball combination shot
impossible you say? . . . hard to believe?, perhaps
out of the realm of possibility? naaaa
he be stretchin' out long tawny fingers out across a
cool green felt with a provocative golden gate
and a full table railshot that's no sweat and I leaned
up against my bannister and wandered over to the
Wurlitzer and I punched A-2 I was lookin' for
something like Wine, Wine, Wine by the Night Caps
starring Chuck E. Weiss or High Blood Pressure
by George (cryin' in the streets) Perkins—no dice
"that's life," that's what all the people say ridin' high

in April, seriously shot down in May, but I know I'm
gonna change that tune when I'm standing underneath
a buttery moon that's all melted off to one side
It was just about that time that the sun
came crawlin' yellow out of a manhole
at the foot of 23rd Street
and a dracula moon in a black disguise
was making its way back to its
pre-paid room at the St. Moritz Hotel [scat]
and the El train came tumbling
across the trestles and it sounded
like the ghost of Gene Krupa
with an overhead cam and glasspacks
and the whispering brushes of wet radials
on a wet pavement and there's a
traffic jam session on Belmont tonight
and the rhapsody of the pending
evening, I leaned up against
my bannister and I've been looking
for some kind of an emotional
investment with romantic dividends
kind of a physical negotiation
is underway
as I attempt to consolidate all my
missed weekly payments, into
one-low-monthly payment
through the nose
with romantic residuals and leg akimbo
but the chances are more than likely I'll probably
be held over for another smashed weekend

Warm Beer and Cold Women

warm beer and cold women, I just don't fit in
every joint I stumbled into tonight
that's just how it's been
all these double knit strangers with
gin and vermouth and recycled stories
in the naugahyde booths

with the platinum blondes
and tobacco brunettes
I'll be drinkin' to forget you
lite another cigarette
and the band's playin' something
by Tammy Wynette
and the drinks are on me tonight

all my conversations I'll just be
talkin' about you baby
borin' some sailor as I try to get through
I just want him to listen
that's all you have to do
he said I'm better off without you
till I showed him my tattoo

now the moon's rising
ain't got no time to lose
time to get down to drinking
tell the band to play the blues
drinks are on me, I'll buy another round
at the last ditch attempt saloon

warm beer and cold women, I just don't fit in
every joint I stumbled into tonight

that's just how it's been
all these double knit strangers with
gin and vermouth and recycled stories
in the naugahyde booths

with the platinum blondes
and tobacco brunettes
I'll be drinking to forget you
lite another cigarette
and the band's playing somethin'
by Johnnie Barnett
and the drinks are on me tonight

I guess things were always quiet
around Putnam County
kind of shy and sleepy as it clung to the skirts
of the 2-lane, that was stretched out like an
asphalt dance floor where all the oldtimers would
hunker down in bib jeans and store bought boots
lyin' about their lives and the places that they'd been
suckin' on Coca Colas and be spittin' Days Work
they's be suckin' on Coca Colas
and be spittin' Day's Work
until the moon was a stray dog on the ridge and
the taverns would be swollen until the naked eye
of 2am, and the Stratocaster guitars slung over
Burgermeister beer guts, and the swizzle stick legs
jacknifed over naugahyde stools and the
witch hazel spread out over the linoleum floors,
the pedal pushers stretched out over midriff bulge
and the coiffed brunette curls over Maybelline eyes
wearing Prince Machiavelli, Estee Lauder,
smells so sweet
I elbowed up at the counter with mixed feelings
over mixed drinks
and Bubba and the Roadmasters moaned in pool hall
concentration as they knit their brows to
cover the entire Hank Williams Song Book
and the old National register was singing to the
tune of $57.57
until last call, one last game of 8 ball
and Berneice would be putting the chairs on the tables,
someone come in say "Hey man, anyone got
any Jumper Cables, is that a 6 or a 12 volt?"
and all the studs in town would toss 'em down

and claim to fame as they stomped their feet
boasting about being able to get more ass
than a toilet seat.
And the GMCs and the Straight 8 Fords
were coughing and wheezing and they
perculated as they tossed the gravel
underneath the fenders to weave home
a wet slick anaconda of a two lane
with tire irons and crowbars a rattlin'
with a tool box and a pony saddle
you're grinding gears, shifting into first
yea and that goddam tranny's just getting worse
with the melodies of "see ya later"
and screwdrivers on carburettors
talkin' shop about money to loan
and palominos and strawberry roans
See ya tomorrow, hello to the Mrs.
money to borrow and goodnight kisses
the radio spittin' out Charlie Rich
sure can sing that sonofabitch
and you weave home, weavin' home
leaving the little joint winking in the
dark warm narcotic American night
beneath a pin cushion sky and it's
home to toast and honey, start
up the Ford, your lunch money's there on the
draining board, toilet's runnin' shake the
handle, telephone's ringin' it's Mrs. Randal
where the hell are my goddam sandals
and the porcelain poodles and the glass swans
staring down from the knick knack shelf
with the parent permission slips for the

kids' field trips
pair of Muckalucks scraping across
the shag carpet
and the impending squint of
first light, that lurked behind
a weeping marquee in downtown Putnam
and would be pullin' up any minute now
just like a bastard amber
Velveeta yellow cab on a rainy corner
and be blowin' its horn, in every window
in town.

Spare Parts I (A Nocturnal Emission)
(by Tom Waits and Chuck E. Weiss)

well the damn cracked hard just like a bull whip
cause it wasn't takin' no lip from the night before
as it shook out the street, the stew bums showed up
just like bounced checks, rubbin' their necks
and the sky turned the color of Pepto-Bismol
and the parking lots growled
and my old sports coat full of promissory notes
and a receipt from a late night motel
and the hawk had his whole family out
there in the wind, and he's got a message
for you to beware cause he be kickin' your
ass in, in a cold blooded fashion
dishin' out more than a good man can bear
I got shoes untied, shirttail's out, ain't got a
ghost of a chance with this old romance
just an apartment for rent down the block
Ivar Theater with live burlesque
and the manager's scowlin', feet on his desk
boom boom against the curtain
you're still hurtin'
and then push came to shove, shove came to biff
girls like that just lay you out stiff
maybe I'll go to Cleveland or
get me a tattoo or somethin', my brother
in law's there
skid mark tattoo on the asphalt blue
was that a Malibu
Liz Taylor and Montgomery Clift
cumming on to the broads with the
same ol' riff. Hey baby come up to
my place, we'll listen to some
smooth music on the stereo, no thank you

got any Stan Getz records
no I got Smothers Brothers
so I combed back my Detroit
jack up my pegs, wiped my Stacy Adams
jacknifed my legs, yea I got designs
on a moving violation
hey baby, you put me on hold and I'm
out in the wind and it's getting
mighty cold . . .
colder than a gut shot bitch wolf dog
with 9 sucking pups pullin' a 4 trap
up a hill in the dead of winter
in the middle of a snowstorm
with a mouth full of porcupine quills

[scat]

yea well I don't need you baby
It's a well known fact
I'm 4 sheets to the wind
I'm glad you're gone
I'm glad you're gone
I'm finally alone
glad you're gone, but I
wish you'd come home
and I struggled out of bed
cause the dawn was crackin' hard like a bullwhip
cause it wasn't takin' no lip from the night before
as it shook out the streets the stew bums
showed up just like bounced checks
rubbin' their necks, and the sky turned the
color of Pepto-Bismol

and my old sports coat full of promissory notes
and the hawk had his whole family out there
in the wind, he got a message for you to beware
kickin' your ass in, in a cold blooded fashion
he be dishin' out more than a good man can bear
well hey baby let's take it to Bakersfield
get a little apartment somewhere

Nobody

Nobody, Nobody
will ever love you
the way I could love you
cause nobody is that strong
love is bitter sweet
and life's treasures deep
but no one can keep
a love that's gone wrong

Nobody, Nobody
will ever love you
the way I could love you
cause nobody's that strong
cause nobody's that strong

Nobody, Nobody
will ever love you
the way I could love you
cause nobody is that strong
you've had many lovers
you'll have many others
but they'll only just break
your poor heart in two

Nobody, Nobody
will ever love you
the way I could love you
cause nobody's that strong
cause nobody's that strong

SMALL
CHANGE

Tom Traubert's Blues

Wasted and wounded, it ain't what the moon did
I've got what I paid for now
see ya tomorrow, hey Frank, can I borrow
a couple of bucks from you, to go
Waltzing Mathilda, waltzing Mathilda, you'll go waltzing
Mathilda with me

I'm an innocent victim of a blinded alley
and I'm tired of all these soldiers here
no one speaks English, and everything's broken
and my Stacys are soaking wet
to go waltzing Mathilda, waltzing Mathilda, you'll go waltzing Mathilda
    with me

now the dogs are barking
and the taxi cab's parking
a lot they can do for me
I begged you to stab me
you tore my shirt open
and I'm down on my knees tonight
Old Bushmill's I staggered, you buried the dagger in
your silhouette window light go to go
waltzing Mathilda, waltzing Mathilda, you'll go waltzing
Mathilda with me

now I lost my Saint Christopher now that I've kissed her and the one-
    armed bandit knows, and the maverick
Chinamen, and the cold-blooded signs
and the girls down by the strip-tease shows go
waltzing Mathilda, waltzing Mathilda, you'll go waltzing Mathilda
    with me

no, I don't want your sympathy, the fugitives say that the streets aren't for
    dreaming now
manslaughter dragnets and the ghosts that sell memories
they want a piece of the action anyhow go
waltzing Mathilda, waltzing Mathilda, you'll go waltzing Mathilda
    with me

and you can ask any sailor, and the keys from the jailor
and the old men in wheelchairs know
that Mathilda's the defendant, she killed about a hundred
and she follows wherever you may go
waltzing Mathilda, waltzing Mathilda, you'll go waltzing
Mathilda with me

and it's a battered old suitcase to a hotel someplace
and a wound that will never heal
no prima donna, the perfume is on
an old shirt that is stained with blood and whiskey
and goodnight to the street sweepers
the night watchman flame keepers
and goodnight to Mathilda too

Step Right Up

Step right up
step right up
step right up
Everyone's a winner, bargains galore
That's right, you too can be the proud owner
Of the quality goes in before the name goes on
One-tenth of a dollar
one-tenth of a dollar
we got service after sales
You need perfume? we got perfume
how 'bout an engagement ring?
Something for the little lady
something for the little lady
Something for the little lady, hmm
Three for a dollar
We got a year-end clearance, we got a white sale
And a smoke-damaged furniture
you can drive it away today
Act now, act now
and receive as our gift, our gift to you
They come in all colors, one size fits all
No muss, no fuss, no spills
you're tired of kitchen drudgery
Everything must go
going out of business
going out of business
Going out of business sale
Fifty percent off original retail price
skip the middle man
Don't settle for less
How do we do it?
how do we do it?

volume, volume, turn up the volume
Now you've heard it advertised, don't hesitate
Don't be caught with your drawers down
Don't be caught with your drawers down
You can step right up, step right up

That's right, it filets, it chops
It dices, slices, never stops
lasts a lifetime, mows your lawn
And it mows your lawn
and it picks up the kids from school
It gets rid of unwanted facial hair
it gets rid of embarrassing age spots
It delivers a pizza
and it lengthens, and it strengthens
And it finds that slipper that's been at large
under the chaise longe for several weeks
And it plays a mean Rhythm Master
It makes excuses for unwanted lipstick on your collar
And it's only a dollar, step right up
it's only a dollar, step right up

'Cause it forges your signature.
If not completely satisfied
mail back unused portion of product
For complete refund of price of purchase
Step right up
Please allow thirty days for delivery
don't be fooled by cheap imitations
You can live in it, live in it
laugh in it, love in it
Swim in it, sleep in it

Live in it, swim in it
laugh in it, love in it
Removes embarrassing stains from contour sheets
that's right
And it entertains visiting relatives
it turns a sandwich into a banquet
Tired of being the life of the party?
Change your shorts
change your life
change your life
Change into a nine-year-old Hindu boy
get rid of your wife
And it walks your dog, and it doubles on sax
Doubles on sax, you can jump back Jack
see you later alligator
See you later alligator
And it steals your car
It gets rid of your gambling debts, it quits smoking
It's a friend, and it's a companion
And it's the only product you will ever need
Follow these easy assembly instructions
it never needs ironing
Well it takes weights off hips, bust
thighs, chin, midriff
Gives you dandruff, and it finds you a job
it is a job
And it strips the phone company free
take ten for five exchange
And it gives you denture breath
And you know it's a friend, and it's a companion
And it gets rid of your traveler's checks
It's new, it's improved, it's old-fashioned

Well it takes care of business
never needs winding
Never needs winding
never needs winding
Gets rid of blackheads, the heartbreak of psoriasis
Christ, you don't know the meaning of heartbreak, buddy
C'mon, c'mon, c'mon, c'mon
'Cause it's effective, it's defective
it creates household odors
It disinfects, it sanitizes for your protection
It gives you an erection
it wins the election
Why put up with painful corns any longer?
It's a redeemable coupon, no obligation
no salesman will visit your home
We got a jackpot, jackpot, jackpot
prizes, prizes, prizes, all work guaranteed
How do we do it
how do we do it
how do we do it
how do we do it
We need your business
we're going out of business
We'll give you the business
Get on the business
end of our going-out-of-business sale
Receive our free brochure, free brochure
Read the easy-to-follow assembly instructions
batteries not included
Send before midnight tomorrow, terms available
Step right up
step right up

step right up
You got it buddy: the large print giveth
and the small print taketh away
Step right up
you can step right up
you can step right up
C'mon step right up
(Get away from me kid, you bother me . . .)
Step right up, step right up, step right up
c'mon, c'mon, c'mon, c'mon, c'mon
Step right up
you can step right up
c'mon and step right up
C'mon and step right up

Jitterbug Boy

Well, I'm a jitterbug boy
by the shoe-shine
resting on my laurels
and my Hardys too
life of Riley on a swing shift
gears follow my drift
Once upon a time I was
in show-biz too

I seen the Brooklyn Dodgers
playin at Ebbets Field
seen the Kentucky Derby too
it's fast women, slow horses, I'm reliable sources
and I'm holding up a lamp post
if you want to know
I seen the Wabash Cannonball,
buddy, I've done it all

beause I slept with the lions
and Marilyn Monroe
had breakfast in the eye
of a hurricane
fought Rocky Marciano,
played Minnesota Fats
burned hundred-dollar bills,

I eaten Mulligan stew
got drunk with Louis Armstrong
what's that old song?
I taught Mickey Mantle
everything that he knows

and so you ask me
what I'm doing here
holding up a lamp post
flippin this quarter,
trying to make up my mind
and if it's heads I'll go to
Tennessee, and tails I'll buy a drink
if it lands on the edge
I'll keep talking to you

I Wish I Was in New Orleans

Well, I wish I was in New Orleans
I can see it in my dreams
arm-in-arm down Burgundy
a bottle and my friends and me
hoist up a few tall cool ones
play some pool and listen to that
tenor saxophone calling me home
and I can hear the band begin
"When the Saints Go Marching In"
by the whiskers on my chin
New Orleans, I'll be there

I'll drink you under the table
be red nose go for walks
the old haunts what I wants
is red beans and rice
and wear the dress I like so well
and meet me at the old saloon
make sure there's a Dixie moon
New Orleans, I'll be there

and deal the cards roll the dice
if it ain't that ole Chuck E. Weiss
and Clayborn Avenue me and you
Sam Jones and all
and I wish I was in New Orleans
I can see it in my dreams
arm-in-arm down Burgundy
a bottle and my friends and me
New Orleans, I'll be there

The Piano Has Been Drinking

The piano has been drinking
my necktie is asleep
and the combo went back to New York
the jukebox has to take a leak
and the carpet needs a haircut
and the spotlight looks like a prison break
'cause the telephone's out of cigarettes
and the balcony's on the make
and the piano has been drinking
the piano has been drinking . . .

and the menus are all freezing
and the lightman's blind in one eye
and he can't see out of the other
and the piano-tuner's got a hearing aid
and he showed up with his mother
and the piano has been drinking
the piano has been drinking

cause the bouncer is a Sumo wrestler
cream puff casper milk toast
and the owner is a mental midget
with the I.Q. of a fencepost
'cause the piano has been drinking
the piano has been drinking . . .

and you can't find your waitress
with a Geiger counter
And she hates you and your friends
and you just can't get served
without her
and the box-office is drooling

and the bar stools are on fire
and the newspapers were fooling
and the ash-trays have retired
the piano has been drinking
the piano has been drinking
The piano has been drinking
not me, not me, not me, not me, not me

Invitation to the Blues

Well she's up against the register
with an apron and a spatula
with yesterday's deliveries,
and the tickets for the bachelors
she's a moving violation
from her conk down to her shoes
but it's just an invitation to the blues

and you feel just like Cagney
looks like Rita Hayworth
at the counter of the Schwab's drug store
you wonder if she might be single
she's a loner likes to mingle
got to be patient and pick up a clue

she says howyougonnalikem
over medium or scrambled
anyway's the only way
be careful not to gamble
on a guy with a suitcase
and a ticket gettin out of here
it's a tired bus station
and an old pair of shoes
but it ain't nothing but an
invitation to the blues

but you can't take your eyes off her
get another cup of java
and it's just the way she pours it for you
joking with the customers
and it's mercy mercy Mr. Percy
there ain't nothin back in Jersey

but a broken-down jalopy of a
man I left behind
and a dream that I was chasin
and a battle with booze
and an open invitation to the blues

but she's had a sugar daddy
and a candy apple Caddy
and a bank account and everything
accustom to the finer things
he probably left her for a socialite
and he didn't love her 'cept at night
and then he's drunk and never
even told her that he cared
so they took the registration
and the car-keys and her shoes
And left her with an invitation
to the blues

'Cause there's a Continental Trailways leaving
local bus tonight, good evening
you can have my seat
I'm stickin round here for a while
get me a room at the Squire
the filling station's hiring
I can eat here every night
what the hell have I got to lose
got a crazy sensation,
go or stay and I've got to choose
and I'll accept your invitation to the blues

Pasties and a G-string

Smelling like a brewery,
looking like a tramp
I ain't got a quarter
got a postage stamp
Been five o'clock shadow boxing
all around the town
Talking with the old men
sleeping on the ground
Bazanti bootin
al zootin al hoot
and Al Cohn
sharin this apartment
with a telephone pole
and it's a fish-net stockings
spike-heel shoes
Strip tease, prick tease
car kease blues
and the porno floor show
live nude girls
dreamy and creamy
and the brunette curls
Chesty Morgan and a
Watermelon Rose
raise my rent and take off
all your clothes
with the trench coats
magazines bottle full of rum
she's so good, it make
a dead man cum, with
pasties and a g-string
beer and a shot
Portland through a shot glass

and a Buffalo squeeze
wrinkles and cherry
and twinky and pinky
and FeFe live from Gay Paree
fanfares rim shots
back stage who cares
all this hot burlesque for me

cleavage, cleavage thighs and hips
from the nape of her neck
to the lip stick lips
chopped and channeled
and lowered and louvered
and a cheater slicks
and baby moons
she's hot and ready
and creamy and sugared
and the band is awful
and so are the tunes

crawlin on her belly shakin like jelly
and I'm getting harder than
Chinese algebraziers and cheers
from the compendium here
hey sweet heart they're yellin for more
squashing out your cigarette butts
on the floor
and I like Shelly
you like Jane
what was the girl with the snake skins name
it's an early bird matinee
come back any day

getcha little sompin
that cha can't get at home
getcha little sompin
that cha can't get at home
pasties and a g-string
beer and a shot
Portland through a shot glass
and a Buffalo squeeze
popcorn, front row
higher than a kite
and I'll be back tomorrow night
and I'll be back tomorrow night

Bad Liver and a Broken Heart

Well I got a bad liver and a broken heart
yea I drunk me a river since you tore me apart
and I don't have a drinking problem
'cept when I can't get a drink
And I wish you'd a known her
we were quite a pair
she was sharp as a razor
and soft as a prayer
so welcome to the continuing saga
she was my better half
and I was just a dog
and so here am I slumped
I been chippied I been chumped
on my stool
so buy this fool, some spirits and libations
it's these railroad station bars
with all these conductors and the porters
and I'm all out of quarters
and this epitaph is the aftermath
yea I choose my path
hey come on Cath, he's a lawyer,
he ain't the one for ya
and no the moon ain't romantic
it's intimidating as hell
and some guy's trying to sell
me a watch
And so I'll meet you at the
bottom of a bottle of
bargain Scotch
I got me a bottle and a dream
it's so maudlin it seems

you can name your poison
go on ahead and make some noise
I ain't sentimental
this ain't a purchase it's a rental
and it's purgatory, hey
what's your story, well
I don't even care
'cause I got my own double-cross to bear

and I'll see your Red Label
and I'll raise you one more
and you can pour me a cab,
I just can't drink no more
'cause it don't douse the flames
that are started by dames
It ain't like asbestos
it don't do nothing but
rest us assured
and substantiate the rumors
that you've heard.

The One That Got Away

The jigolo's jumpin salty
ain't no trade out on the streets
half past the unlucky
and the hawk's a front-row seat
dressed in full orquestration
stage door johnnys got to pay
and sent him home
talking bout the one that got away

could a been on easy street
could a been a wheel
with irons in the fire
and all them business deals
But the last of the big-time losers
shouted before he drove away
I'll be right back as soon as I crack
the one that got away

the ambulance drivers don't give a shit
they just want to get off work
and the short stop and the victim
have already gone berserk
and the shroud-tailor measures him
for a deep-six holiday
the stiff is froze, the case is closed
on the one that got away

Jim Crow's directing traffic
with them cemetery blues
with them peculiar looking trousers
them old Italian shoes

the wooden kimona was all ready
to drop in San Francisco Bay
but now he's mumbling something
all about the one that got away

Costello was the champion
at the St. Moritz Hotel
and the best this side of Fairfax,
reliable sources tell
but his reputation is at large
and he's at Ben Frank's every day
waiting for the one that got away

he's got a snake skin sportshirt,
and he looks like Vincent Price
with a little piece of chicken
and he's carving off a slice
but someone tipped her off
she'll be doing a Houdini now any day
she shook his hustle
and a Greyhound bus'll
take the one that got away

Andre is at the piano
behind the Ivar in the sewers
with a buck a shot for pop tunes,
and a fin for guided tours
He could of been in Casablanca
he stood in line out there all day
but now he's spilling whiskey
and learning songs about a one that got away

well I've lost my equilibrium
my car keys and my pride
tattoo parlor's warm
and so I huddle there inside
the grinding of the buzz saw
whatchuwanthathingtosay
just don't misspell her name
buddy she's the one that got away

Small Change (Got Rained on with His Own .38)

Well small change got rained on with his own .38
and nobody flinched down by the arcade
and the marquise weren't weeping
they went stark-raving mad
and the cabbies were the only ones
that really had it made
and his cold trousers were twisted,
and the sirens high and shrill
and crumpled in his fist was a five-dollar bill
and the naked mannikins with their
cheshire grins
and the raconteurs
and roustabouts said buddy
come on in
cause the dreams ain't broken down here now
now ... they're walking with a limp
now that

small change got rained on with his own .38
and nobody flinched down by the arcade
and the burglar alarm's been disconnected
and the newsmen start to rattle
and the cops are tellin' jokes
about some whore house in Seattle
and the fire hydrants plead the 5th Amendment
and the furniture's bargains galore
but the blood is by the jukebox
on an old linoleum floor
and it's a hot rain on 42nd Street
and now the umbrellas ain't got a chance
And the newsboy's a lunatic
with stains on his pants cause

small change got rained on with his own .38
and no one's gone over to close his eyes
and there's a racing form in his pocket
circled "Blue Boots" in the 3rd
and the cashier at the clothing store
he didn't say a word as the
siren tears the night in half
and someone lost his wallet
well it's surveillance of assailants
if that's whatchawannacallit
and the whores hike up their skirts
and fish for drug-store prophylactics*
with their mouths cut just like
razor blades and their eyes are like stilettos
and her radiator's steaming
and her teeth are in a wreck
now she won't let you kiss her
but what the hell do you expect
and the Gypsies are tragic and if you
wanna to buy perfume, well
they'll bark you down like
carneys . . . sell you Christmas cards in June
but . . .

small change got rained on with his own .38
and his headstone's
a gumball machine
no more chewing gum
or baseball cards or

---

* This line omitted from lyric sheet.

overcoats or dreams and
someone is hosing down the sidewalk
and he's only in his teens

small change got rained on with his own .38
and a fistful of dollars can't change that
and someone copped his watch fob
and someone got his ring
and the newsboy got his porkpie Stetson hat
and the tuberculosis old men
at the Nelson wheeze and cough
and someone will head south
until this whole thing cools off cause
small change got rained on with his own .38
yea small change got rained on with his own .38

I Can't Wait to Get Off Work (And See My Baby on Montgomery Avenue)

Well I don't mind working
cause I used to be jerkin off
most of my time in the bars
I been a cabbie and a stock clerk
and a soda fountain jock jerk
and a manic mechanic on cars
It's nice work if you can get it
now who the hell said it
I got money to spend on my gal
but the work never stops
and I'll be busting my chops
working for Joe and Sal.

And I can't wait to get off work
and see my baby
she said she'd leave the porch lite
on for me
I'm disheveled I'm disdainful
and I'm distracted and it's painful
but this job sweeping up here is
is gainfully employing me tonight

Tom do this Tom do that
Tom, don't do that
count the cash, clean the oven
dump the trash oh your lovin
is a rare and a copasetic gift
and I'm a moonlight watchmanic
it's hard to be romantic
(sweeping up over by the
cigarette machine
sweeping up over by the cigarette machine . . .)

I can't wait to get off work
and see my baby
she'll be waiting up with a magazine for me
clean the bathrooms, clean um good
oh your lovin I wish you would
come down here and sweepameoffmyfeet
this broom'll have to be my baby
if I hurry, I just might
get off before the dawns early light.

FOREIGN AFFAIRS

Muriel

muriel since you left town the clubs closed down
and there's one more burned out lamppost down on the main street
down where we used to stroll

and muriel i still hit all the same old haunts
and you follow me wherever i go
and muriel i see you on a saturday night
in a penny arcade with your hair tied back
and the diamond twinkle in your eye
is the only wedding ring i'll buy you
muriel

and muriel how many times i've left this town
to hide from your memory
and it haunts me
but i only get as far as the next whiskey bar
i buy another cheap cigar and i'll see you every night
hey muriel muriel
hey buddy got a light

I Never Talk To Strangers

stop me if you've heard this one
i feel as though we've met before
perhaps i'm mistaken
but it's just that i remind you
of someone you used to care about
but that was long ago
do you think i'd fall for that
i wasn't born yesterday
besides i never talk to strangers anyway

i ain't a bad guy when you get to know me
i just thought there ain't no harm
hey just try minding your own business
bud who asked you to annoy me
with your sad repartee
besides i never talk to strangers anyway
your life's a dimestore novel

this town is full of guys like you
and you're looking for someone to take the place of her
and you're bitter cause he left you
that's why you're drinkin in this bar
well only suckers fall in love
with perfect strangers

it always takes one to know one stranger
maybe we're just wiser now
and been around the block so many times
that we don't notice
that we're all just perfect strangers
as long as we ignore

that we all begin as strangers
just before we find
we really aren't strangers anymore

Jack & Neal

jack was sittin poker faced with bullets backed with bitches
neal hunched at the wheel puttin everyone in stitches
braggin bout this nurse he screwed while drivin through nebraska
and when she came she honked the horn and neal just barely missed a
truck and then he asked her if she'd like to come like that to californy
see a red head in a uniform will always get you horny
with her hairnet and those white shoes and a name tag and a hat
she drove like andy granatelli and knew how to fix a flat
and jack was almost at the bottom of his md 2020 neal was yellin
out the window tryin to buy some bennies from a lincoln
full of mexicans whose left rear tire blowed and the sonsobitches
prit near almost ran off the road

well the nurse had spilled the manoshevitz all up and down her dress
then she lit the map on fire neal just had to guess
should we try and find a bootleg route or a fillin station open
the nurse was dumpin out her purse lookin for an envelope and
jack was out of cigarettes we crossed the yellow line
the gas pumps looked like tombstones from here
felt lonelier than a parking lot when the last car pulls away
and the moonlight dressed the double breasted foothills
in the mirror weaving outa negligee and a black brassiere
the mercury was runnin hot and almost out of gas
just then florence nightingale dropped her drawers and
stuck her fat ass half way out of the window with a
wilson pickett tune
and shouted get a load of this and gave the finger to the moon

countin one eyed jacks and whistling dixie in the car
neal was doin least a hundred when we saw a fallin star
florence wished that neal would hold her stead of chewin

his cigar jack was noddin out and dreamin he was in a bar
with charlie parker on the bandstand not a worry in the world
and a glass of beer in one hand and his arm around a girl
and neal was singin to the nurse
underneath a harlem moon
and somehow you could just tell we'd be in california soon

A Sight For Sore Eyes

hey sight for sore eyes it's a long time no see
workin hard hardly workin hey man you know me
water under the bridge didya see my new car
well it's bought and it's payed for parked outside of the bar

and hey barkeeper what's keepin you keep pourin drinks
for all these palookas hey you know what i thinks
that we toast to the old days and dimagio too
and old drysdale and mantle whitey ford and to you

no the old gang ain't around everyone has left town
'cept for thumm and giardina said they just might be down
oh half drunk all the time and i'm all drunk the rest
yea monk's till the champion but i'm the best

i guess you heard about nash he was killed in a crash
hell that must of been two or three years ago now
yea he spun out and he rolled he hit a telephone pole
and he died with the radio on
no she's married and with a kid finally split up with sid
he's up north for a nickle's worth for armed robbery

hey i'll play you some pin ball hell you ain't got a chance
well then go on over and ask her to dance

Potter's Field

(by Tom Waits and Bob Alcivar)

well you can buy me a drink and i'll tell you what i seen
and i'll give you a bargain from the edge of a maniac's dream
that buys a black widow spider with a riddle in his yarn
that's clinging to the furrow of a blindman's brow
i'll start talking from the brim of a thimble full of whiskey
on a train through the bronx that will take you just as far
as the empty of a bottle to the highway of a scar
that stretched across the blacktop of my cheek like that
and then ducks beneath the brim of a fugitive's hat
and you'll learn why liquor makes a stool pigeon rat on every face
that ever left his shadow down on saint marks place

hell i'd double cross my mother if it was whiskey that they payed
and so an early bird says nightsticks on the hit parade
and he ain't got a prayer and his days are numbered
and you'll track him down like a dog
well it's a tough customer you're getting in this trade
cause the nightstick's heart pumps lemonade
well whiskey keeps a blindman talkin alright
and i'm the only one who knows just where he stayed last night

he was in a wreckin yard in a switchblade storm
in a wheelbarrow with nothing but revenge to keep him warm
and a half a million dollars in unmarked bills
was the nightstick's blanket in a febuary chill
and as the buzzard drove a crooked sky
he was dealin high chicago in the mud
and stackin' the deck against a dragnet's eye
a shivering nightstick in a miserable heap
with the siren for a lullaby singing him to sleep
he was bleeding from a buttonhole
torn by a slug fired from the barrel of a two dollar gun

that scorched a blister on the grip of a punk by now
is learnin what you have to pay to be a hero anyhow

he dressed the hole in his gut with a hundred dollar bandage
a king's ransom for a bedspread that don't amount to nuttin
just cobweb strings on a busted ukulele
and the nightstick leaned on a black shillelagh
with the poison of a junkie's broken promise on his lip

he staggered in the shadows screaming i ain't never been afraid
and he shot out every street light on the promenade
past the frozen ham and eggers at the penny arcade
throwin out handfuls of a blood stained salary
they were dead in their tracks at the shootin gallery
and they fired off a twenty one gun salute
and from the corner of his eye he caught the alabaster orbs
and from a dime a dance hall girl and stuffed a thousand dollar bill
in her blouse and caught the cruel and unusual punishment of her smile
and the nightstick winked beneath a rainsoaked brim
ain't no one seen hide nor hair of him see
no one but a spade on rikers island and me
and so if you're mad enough to listen to a full of whiskey blindman
then you're mad enough to look beyond where bloodhounds dare to go
so if you want to know just where the nightstick's hidin out
you be down at the ferry landin oh let's say bout half past a nightmare
when it's twisted on a clock you tell 'em nickels sentcha
whiskey always makes him talk
and you ask for captain charon with the mud on his kicks
he's the skipper of the deadline steamer
and she sails from the bronx across the river styx
and a riddle's just a ticket for a dreamer

'cause when the weathervane's sleepin and the moon turns his back
you crawl on your belly long the railroad tracks
and cross your heart and hope to die and stick a needle in your eye
cause he'd cut my bleedin heart out if he found out that i squealed
cause you see a scarecrow's just a hoodlum
who marked the cards that he dealed
and pulled a gypsy switch
out on the edge of potter's field

Burma Shave

licorice tattoo turned a gun metal blue scrawled across the shoulders
of a dying town the one eyed jacks across the railroad tracks
and the scar on its belly pulled a stranger passing through
he was a juvenile delinquent never learned how to behave
but the cops would never think to look in
burma shave

and the road was like a ribbon and the moon was like a bone
he didn't seem to be like any guy she'd ever known
he kinda looked like farley granger with his hair slicked back
she says i'm a sucker for a fella in a cowboy hat
how far are you going he said depends on what you mean
he says i'm going thataway just as long as it's paved
i guess you'd say i'm on my way to
burma shave

and her knees up on the glove compartment
took out her barrettes and her hair spilled out like rootbeer
and she popped her gum and arched her back
hell marysville ain't nothing but a wide spot in the road
some night my heart pounds just like thunder
i don't know why it don't explode
cause everyone in this stinking town has got one foot in the grave
and i'd rather take my chances out in
burma shave

presley's what i go by why don't you change the station
count the grain elevators in the rearview mirror
mister anywhere you point this thing
has got to beat the hell out of the sting
of going to bed with every dream that dies here every mornin
and so drill me a hole with a barber pole

i'm jumping my parole just like a fugitive tonight
why don't you have another swig
and pass that car if you're so brave
i wanna get there before the sun comes up in
burma shave

and the spider web crack and the mustang screamed
smoke from the tires and the twisted machine
just a nickel's worth of dreams and every wishbone that they saved
lie swindled from them on the way to
burma shave

and the sun hit the derrick and cast a bat wing shadow
up against the car door on the shot gun side
and when they pulled her from the wreck you know she
still had on her shades
they say that dreams are growing wild just this side of
burma shave

Barber Shop

good mornin mr. snip snip snip witchur haircut jus as short as mine
bay rum lucky tiger butch wax cracker jacks shoe shine jaw breaker
magazine racks hangin round the barber shop a side burnin close crop
mornin mr. furgeson what's the good word witcha been
stayin outa trouble like a good boy should i see you're still cuttin hair
well i'm still cuttin classes i just couldn't hep myself
i got a couple of passes to the ringle bros. barn bail circus afternoon
i see you lost a little round the middle and your lookin reel good
sittin on the wagon stead of under the hood
what's the low down mr. brown heard you boy's leavin town
i just bought myself a struggle buggy suckers powder blue
throw me over sports page cincinnati's lookin' good
always been for pittsburgh lay you 10 to 1
that the pirates get the pennant and the series for their done
you know the hair's gettin longer and the skirts gettin shorter
you can get a cheaper haircut if you wanna cross the border
now if your mama saw you smokin why she'd kick your ass
put it out you little juvenile and put it out fast
oh if i had a million dollars well what would i do
probly be a barber not a bum like you
still gotchur paper route now that's just fine
now you can pay me double cause you gypped me last time
you be keepin little circus money and spend it on a girl
know i give the best haircuts in the whole wide world

Foreign Affair

when travelling abroad in the continental style
it's my belief one must attempt to be discreet
and subsequently bear in mind your transient position
allows you a perspective that's unique
though you'll find your itinerary's a blessing and a curse
your wanderlust won't let you settle down
and you'll wonder how you ever fathomed that you'd be content
to stay within the city limits of a small midwestern town
most vagabonds i knowed don't ever want to find the culprit
that remains the object of their long relentless quest
the obsession's in the chasing and not the apprehending
the pursuit you see and never the arrest

without fear of contradiction bon voyage is always hollered
in conjunction with a handkerchief from shore
by a girl that drives a rambler and furthermore
is overly concerned that she won't see him anymore
planes and trains and boats and buses
characteristically evoke a common attitude of blue
unless you have a suitcase and a ticket and a passport
and the cargo that they're carrying is you
a foreign affair juxtaposed with a stateside
and domestically approved romantic fancy
is mysteriously attractive due to circumstances knowing
it will only be parlayed into a memory

BLUE
VALENTINE

Red Shoes by the Drugstore

She wore red shoes by the drugstore
as the rain splashed the nickel
spilled like chablis along the midway
theres a little bluejay
in a red dress, on a sad night

one straw in a rootbeer
a compact with a cracked mirror
and a bottle of evening in paris perfume

he told her to wait in by the magazines
he had to take care of some buisness it seems
bring a raincoat and a suitcase
and your dark eyes
and wear those red shoes

theres a dark huddle at the bus stop
umbrellas arranged in a sad bouquet
li'l cesaer got caught
he was going down to second
he was cooled
changing stations on the chamber
to steal a diamond
from a jewelry store for his baby
he loved the way she looked in those red shoes

she waited by the drugstore
cesaer had never been this late before
and the dogs bayed the moon
and rattled their chains
and the cold jingle of taps in a puddle
was the burglar alarm
snitchin on ceasar

now the rain washes memories from the sidewalks
and the hounds splash down the nickel
full of soldiers
and santa claus is drunk in the ski room
and it's christmas eve in a sad cafe
when the moon gets this way
there's a little blue jay
by the newstand
wearing red shoes

so meet me tonight by the drugstore
we're goin out tonight
wear your red shoes

Christmas Card from a Hooker
in Minneapolis

hey charlie i'm pregnant
and living on the 9th street
right above a dirty bookstore
off euclid avenue
and i stopped takin dope
and i quit drinkin whiskey
and my old man plays the trombone
and works out at the track

and he says that he loves me
even though its not his baby
and he says that he'll raise him up
like he would his own son
and he gave me a ring
that was worn by his mother
and he takes me out dancin
every saturday night.

and hey charlie i think about you
everytime i pass a fillin station
om account of all the grease
you used to wear in your hair
and i still have that record
of little anthony & the imperials
but someone stole my record player
now how do you like that?

hey charlie i almost went crazy
after mario got busted
so i went back to omaha to
live with my folks
but everyone i used to know

was either dead or in prison
so i came back to minneapolis
this time i think i'm gonna stay.

hey charlie i think i'm happy
for the first time since my accident
and i wish i had all the money
that we used to spend on dope
i'd buy me a used car lot
and i wouldn't sell any of 'em
i'd just drive a different car
every day, dependin on how
i feel

hey charlie for chrissakes
do you want to know the
truth of it?
i don't have a husband
he don't play the trombone
and i need to borrow money
to pay this lawyer
and charlie, hey
i'll be eligible for parole
come valentines day

Romeo is Bleeding

romeo is bleeding but not so as you'd notice
he's over on 18th street as usual
looking so hatd against the hood of his car
ans putting out a cigarette in his hand
and for all the pachucos at the pumps
at romeros paint and body
they all seein how far they can spit
well it was just another night
but now they're huddled in the brake lights of a 58 belair
and listenin how romeo killed a sherif with his knife

and they all jump when they hear the sirens
but romeo just laughs and says
all the racket in the world ain't never gonna
save that coppers ass
he'll never see another summertime
for gunnin down my brother
and leavin him like a dog
beneath a car without his knife

and romeo says hey man gimme a cigatette
and they all reach for their pack
and frankie lights it for him and pats him on the back
and throws a bottle at a milk truck
and as it breaks he grabs his nuts
and they all know they could ve just like romeo
if they only had the guts

but romeo is bleeding but nobody can tell
amd he sings along with the radio
with a bullet in his chest
and he combs back his fenders

and they all agree its clear
that everything is cool now that romeos here
but romeo is bleeding
and he winches now and then and he leans against
the car door and feels the blood in his shoes
and someones crying in the phone booth
at the 5 points by the store
romeo starts his engine
and wipes the blood of the door
and he brodys through the signal
with the radio full blast
leavin the boys there hikin up their chinos
and they all try to stand like romeo
beneath the moon cut like a sickle
and they're talkin now in spanish about their hero

but romeo is bleeding as he gives the man his ticket
and he climbs to the balcony at the movies
and he'll die without a whimper
like every heros dream
just an angel with a bullet
and cagney in the screen

$29.00

little black girl in a red dress
on a hot night with a broken shoe
little black girl you shoulda never left home
theres probly someone thats still waitin up for you
its cold back in chicago
but in los angeles its worse
when all you got is $29.00 and an alligator purse

i see already that vulture in the fleetwood
with the shartruse hood
can see you're trying to get your bearings
and you say hey which ways the main stem
and where ever you say you're from
he'll say he grew up there himself
and he'll comeon and make you feel
like you grew up right next door to him
and you say take a left on central
and he throws it in reverse
'cause you only got $29.00 and an alligator purse

and he'll come on like a gentleman
and you'll be a little shy
you say your ex old man was a sax player
he'll say baby i used to play bass for sly
and you say you like his cadillac,
say honey i got 2 or 3
he'll say sweetheart you're sure fortunate
that you ran into me
when you've done a dime in the joint
you figure nothin could be worse
and you got $29.00 in an alligator purse

well he got pharoh on the 8 track
you start smokin a little boo
you thinkin gettin out of chicago was the
best thing ever happened to you
but he ain't no good samaritan
he'll make sure he's reimbursed
lot more than $29.00 and an alligator purse

now when the streets get hungry, baby
you can almost hear them growl
someone's setting a place for you
when the dogs begin to howl

well the streets are dead
they creep up and ??? but it was left on the pole
they make . . . suckers always make mistakes
when they're far away from home
Chicken in a pot
Whoever gets their first
Gonna get himself 29.00
and an alligator purse

now the sirens just an epilog
the cops always get there too late
they always stop for coffee
on the way to the scene of the crime
they always try so hard to look like movie stars
they couldnt catch a cold
you only wasting your dime
and she's lucky to be alive
the doctor whispered to the nurse
she only lost a 1/2 pint of blood
$29.00 and an alligator purse

Wrong Side of the Road

put a dead cat on the railroad tracks
when the wolf bains blooming by the tressel
and get the eyeball of a rooster
and the stones from a ditch
and wash 'em down with bilge water
and you say you'll never snitch
take the buttons from a yellow jacket
the feafrom a buzzard
and the blood from a bounty hunters cold black heart
catch the tears of a widow
in a thimble made of glass
tell your mama and papa
they can kick your ass
poison all the water in the wishin well
and hang all them scarecrows from a sycamore tree
burn down all those honeymoons
put 'em in a pillow case
and wait next to the switch blades
at the amusement park for me
strangle all the christmas carols
scratch out all your prayers
tie 'em up with barbed wire
and push them down the stairs
and i'll whittle you a pistol
for keeping nightmares of the blinds
those sunabitches always seem to sneak up from behind
syphon all the gas from your daddys pickup truck
fill up johnnys t bird
i got a couple of bucks
put a little perfume and ribbon in your hair
careful that you don't wake up the hounds
tear a bolt of lightning
of the side of the sky

and throw it in the cedar chest
if you want to tell me why
bring the gear shift knob from a 49 merc
and lay down here beside me
let me hold you in the dirt
and you'll tremble as the flames
tear the throat out of the night
sink your teeth into my shoulder
dig your nails into my back
tell that little girl to let go of my sleeve
you'll be a woman when i catch you
as you fall in love with me
then with my double barrel shotgun
and a whole box of shells
we'll celebrate the 4 of july
we'll do 100 mph
spendin someone elses dough
and we'll drive all the way to reno
on the wrong side of the road

Whistlin' Past the Graveyard

well i come in on a night train
with an arm full of box cars
on the wings of a magpie
cross a hooligan night
and i busted up a chifforobe
way out by the cocomo
cooked up a mess a mulligan
and got into a fight

[chorus] whistlin past the graveyard
steppin on a crack
i'm a mean motherhubbard
papa one eyed jack

you propably seen me sleepin
out by the railroad tracks
go on and ask the prince of darkness
what about all thet smoke
come from the stack
sometimes i kill myself a jacket
suck out all the blood
steal myself a stationwagon
drivin through the mud

[chorus]

i know you seen my headlights
and the honkin of my horn
i'm callin out my bloodhounds
chase the devil through the corn
last night i chugged the mississippi
now that suckers dry as a bone

born in a taxi cab
i'm never comin home

[chorus]

my eyes have seen the glory
of the draining of the ditch
i only come to baton rouge
to find myself a witch
i'm-ona snatch me up a
couple of 'em every time it rains
you see a locomotive
probably thinkin its a train

[chorus]

what you think is the sunshine
is just a twinkle in my eye
that ring around my fingers
just the 4th of july
when i get a little bit lonesome
and a tear falls from my cheek
theres gonna be an ocean in
the middle of the week

[chorus]

i rode into town on a night train
with an arm full of box cars
on the wings of a magpie
cross a hooligan night
i'm-ona tear me off a rainbow

and wear it for a tie
i never told the truth
so i can never tell a lie

[chorus]

Kentucky Avenue

eddie graces buick got 4 bullet holes in the side
charlie delisle sittin at the top of an avocado tree
mrs stormll stab you with a steak knife if you step on her lawn i got a half
    pack of lucky strikes
man come along with me lets fill our pockets with macadamia nuts then
    go over to bobby
goodmansons and jump off the roof hilda plays strip poker and her ma-
    mas across the street joey
navinski says she put her tongue in his mouth dicky faulkners got a
    switchblade and some
gooseneck risers that eucalyptus is a hunchback theres a wind up from the
    south let me tie you up
with kite string and i'll show you the scabs on my knee watch out for the
    broken glass, put your
shoes and socks on and come along with me lets follow that fire track
i think your house is burnin down
the go down to the hobo jungle
and kill some rattle snakes with a trowel
we'll break all the windows in the old anderson place
and steal a bunch of boysenberrys
and smear 'em on our face
i'll get a dollar from my mamas purse
and buy that skull and crossbones ring
and you can wear it around your neck
on an old piece of string

then we'll spit on ronnie arnold
and flip him the bird
and slash the tires on the school bus
now don't say a word
i'll take a rusty nail
and scratch your initials on my arm

and i'll show you how to sneak up
on the roof of the drugstore

take the spokes from your wheelchair
and a magpies wings
and tie 'em to your shoulders and your feet
i'll steal a hacksaw from my dad
and cut the braces off your legs
and we'll bury them tonight in the cornfield

put a church key in your pocket
we'll hop that freight train in the hall
and we'll slide down the drain all the way
to new orleans in the fall

A Sweet Little Bullet from a
Pretty Blue Gun

it's raining it's pouring
and you didn't bring a sweater
nebraska will never let you come back home
and on hollywood and wine
by the thrifty mart sign
any night i'll be willin to bet
there's a young girl
with sweet little wishes
and pretty blue dreams
standin there and gettin all wet

now there's a place off the drag
called the gilbert hotel
there's a couple letters burned out in the sign
and it's better than a bus stop
and they do good buisness
every time it rains
for sweet little girls
with nothing in their jeans
but sweet little wishes
and pretty blue dreams

now it's raining it's pouring
the old mam is snoring
now i lay me down to sleep
i hear the sirens in the street
all the dreams are made of chrome
i have no way to get back home
i'd rather die before i wake
like marilyn monroe
and throw my jeans out in
the street and the rain will make 'em grow

now the night clerk he got a club foot
and he's heard every hard luck story
at least a hundred times or more
he says check out time is 10 am
and that's just what he means
and you go up the stairs
with sweet little wishes
and pretty blue dreams

now it's raining it's pouring
and hollywood's just fine
swindle a little out of her dreams
put a letter in the sign
never trust a scarecrow
wearin' shades after dark
be careful of that old bow tie he wears
it takes a sweet little bullet
from a pretty blue gun
to put those scarlet ribbons in your hair

no that ain't no cherry bomb
4th of july's all done
just some fool playin' that second line
from the barrel of a pretty blue gun

no that ain't no cherry bomb
4th of july's all done
just some fool playin' that second line
from the barrel of a pretty blue gun

Blue Valentines

She sends me blue valentines
All the way from Philadelphia
To mark the anniversary
Of someone that I used to be
And it feels just like theres
A warrant out for my arrest
Got me checkin in my rearview mirror
And I'm always on the run
Thats why I changed my name
And I didn't think you'd ever find me here

To send me blue valentines
Like half forgotten dreams
Like a pebble in my shoe
As I walk these streets
And the ghost of your memory
Is the thistle in the kiss
And the burgler that can break a roses neck
It's the tatooed broken promise
That I hide beneath my sleeve
And I see you every time I turn my back

She sends me blue valentines
Though I try to remain at large
They're insisting that our love
Must have a eulogy
Why do I save all of this madness
In the nightstand drawer
There to haunt upon my shoulders
Baby I know
I'd be luckier to walk around everywhere I go
With a blind and broken heart
That sleeps beneath my lapel

She sends me my blue valentines
To remind me of my cardinal sin
I can never wash the guilt
Or get these bloodstains off my hands
And it takes a lot of whiskey
To take this nightmares go away
And I cut my bleedin heart out every nite
And I die a little more on each St. Valentines day
Remember that I promised I would
Write you . . .
These blue valentines
blue valentines
blue valentines

HEARTATTACK AND VINE

Heartattack and Vine

liar liar with your pants on fire,
white spades hangin' on the telephone
wire, gamblers reevaluate along the dotted line,
you'll never recognize
yourself on heartattack and vine.

doctor lawyer beggar man thief,
philly joe remarkable looks on in disbelief,
if you want a taste of madness,
you'll have to wait in line, you'll probably
see someone you know on heartattack and vine.

boney's high on china white, shorty found a punk,
don't you know there ain't
no devil, there's just god when he's drunk,
well this stuff will probably kill
you, let's do another line,
what you say you meet me down
on heartattack and vine.

see that little jersey girl in the see-through top,
with the peddle pushers sucking on a soda pop,
well i bet she's still a virgin
but it's only twenty-five 'til nine,
you can see a million of 'em
on heartattack and vine.

better off in iowa against your scrambled eggs,
than crawling down cahuenga on a broken pair of legs,
you'll find your ignorance is blissful every goddamn time,
your're waitin' for the rtd on heartattack and vine.

Saving All My Love For You

It's too early for the circus,
It's too late for the bars,
no one's sleepin' but the paperboys,
and no one in this town is makin' any noise,
but the dogs and the milkmen and me.

The girls around here all look like cadillacs,
no one likes a stranger here,
I'd come home but i'm afraid
that you won't take me back,
but i'd trade off everything just to have you near.

I know i'm irresponsible and i don't behave,
and i ruin everything that i do,
and i'll probably get arrested when i'm in my grave,
but i'll be savin' all my love for you.

I paid fifteen dollars for a prostitute,
with too much makeup and a broken shoe,
but her eyes were just a counterfeit,
she tried to gyp me out of it,
but you know that i'm still in love you.

Don't listen to the rumors that you hear about me,
cause i ain't as bad as they make me out to be,
well i may lose my mind but baby can't you see,
that i'll be savin' all my love for you.

Downtown

Red pants and the sugarman in the temple street gloom,

drinkin' chivas regal in a four dollar room,
just another dead soldier in a powder blue night,
sugarman says baby everything's alright,
goin' downtown down downtown.

Montclaire de havelin doin' the st. vitus dance,
lookin' for someone to chop the lumber in his pants,
how am i gonna unload all of this ice and all this mink,
all the traffic in the street but it's so hard to think,
goin' downtown down downtown.

Frankie's wearin' lipstick pierre cardin,
i swear to god i seen him holdin' hands with jimmy bond,
sally's high on crank and hungry for some sweets,
she's fem in the sheets but she's butch in the streets,
goin' downtown down downtown.

It's the cool of the evening the sun's goin' down,
i want to hold you in my arms i want to push you around,
i want to break your bottle and spill out all your charms,
come on baby we'll set off all the burglar alarms,
goin' downtown down downtown.

Red pants and the sugarman in the temple street gloom,
drinkin' chivas regal in a four dollar room,
just another dead soldier in a powder blue night,
red pants turns to sugarman and says everything's alright,
goin' downtown down downtown.

Jersey Girl

Got no time for the corner boys,
down in the street makin' all that noise,
don't want no whores on eighth avenue,
cause tonight i'm gonna be with you.
'cause tonight i'm gonna take that ride,

across the river to the jersey side,
take my baby to the carnival,
and i'll take you on all the rides,
sing sha la la la la la sha la la la.

Down the shore everything's alright,
you're with your baby on a saturday night,
don't you know that all my dreams come true,
when i'm walkin' down the street with you,
sing sha la la la la la sha la la la.

You know she thrills me with all her charms,
when i'm wrapped up in my baby's arms,
my little angel gives me everything,
I know someday that she'll wear my ring.

So don't bother me cause i got no time,
I'm on my way to see that girl of mine,
nothin' else matters in this whole wide world,
when you're in love with a jersey girl,
sing sha la la la la la la.

and i call your name, i can't sleep at night,
sha la la la la la la.

'Til the Money Runs Out

check this strange beverage that falls out from the sky,
splashin' bagdad on the hudson in panther martin's eyes,
he's high and outside wearin' candy apple red,
scarlet gave him twenty seven stitches in his head,
with a pint of green chartreuse ain't nothin' seems right,
you buy the sunday paper on a saturday night.

can't you hear the thunder someone stole my watch,
I sold a quart of blood and bought a half a pint of scotch,
some one tell those chinamen on telegraph canyon road,
when you're on the bill with the spoon there ain't no time
to unload, so bye bye baby baby bye bye.

droopy stranger lonely dreamer toy puppy and the prado,
we're laughin' as they piled into olmos' el dorado,
jesus whispered eni meany miney moe,
they're too proud to duck their heads
that's why they bring it down so low,
so bye bye baby baby bye bye.

the pointed man is smack dab in the middle of july,
swingin' from the rafters in his brand new tie,
he said i can't go back to that hotel room
all they do is shout,
but i'll stay wichew baby till the money runs out,
so bye bye baby baby bye bye.

On the Nickel

sticks and stones will break my bones,
but i always will be true, and when
your mama is dead and gone,
i'll sing this lullabye just for you,
and what becomes of all the little boys,
who never comb their hair,
well they're lined up all around the block,
on the nickel over there.

so you better bring a bucket,
there is a hole in the pail,
and if you don't get my letter,
then you'll know that i'm in jail,
and what becomes of all the little boys,
who never say their prayers,
well they're sleepin' like a baby,
on the nickel over there.

and if you chew tobacco, and wish upon a star,
well you'll find out where the scarecrows sit,
just like punchlines between the cars,
and i know a place where a royal flush,
can never beat a pair, and even thomas jefferson,
is on the nickel over there.

so ring around the rosie, you're sleepin' in the rain,
and you're always late for supper,
and man you let me down again,
i thought i heard a mockingbird, roosevelt knows where,
you can skip the light, with grady tuck,
on the nickel over there.

so what becomes of all the little boys,
who run away from home,
well the world just keeps gettin' bigger,
once you get out on your own,
so here's to all the little boys,
the sandman takes you where,
you'll be sleepin' with a pillowman,
on the nickel over there.

so let's climb up through that button hole,
and we'll fall right up the stairs,
and i'll show you where the short dogs grow,
on the nickel over there.

Mr. Siegal

I spent all my money in a mexican whorehouse,
across the street from a catholic church,
and then i wiped off my revolver,
and i buttoned up my burgundy shirt,
i shot the morning in the back,
with my red wings on,
i told the sun he'd better go back down,
and if i can find a book of matches,
i'm goin' to burn this hotel down.

you got to tell me brave captain,
why are the wicked so strong,
how do the angels get to sleep,
when the devil leaves the porchlight on.

well i dropped thirty grand on the nugget slots,
i had to sell my ass on fremont street,
and the drummer said there's sanctuary,
over at the bagdad room,
and now it's one for the money, two for the show,
three to get ready, and go man go,
i said tell me mr. siegel,
how do i get out of here.

well willard's knocked out on a bottle of heat,
drivin' dangerous curves across the dirty sheets,
he said man you ought to see her,
when her parents are gone,
man you ought to hear her when the siren's on.
you got to tell me brave captain,
why are the wicked so strong,
how do the angels get to sleep,
when the devil leaves the porchlight on.

don't you know that ain't no broken bottle,
that i picked up in my headlights,
on the other side of the nevada line,
where they live hard die young,
nd have a good lookin' corpse every time,
well the pit-boss said i should keep movin',
this is where you go when you die,
and so i shot a black beauty,
and i kissed her right between the eyes.

well willard's knocked out on a bottle of heat,
drivin' dangerous curves across the dirty sheets,
he said man you ought to see her,
when her parents are gone,
man you ought to hear her when the siren's on.
you got to tell me brave captain,
why are the wicked so strong,
how do the angels get to sleep,
when the devil leaves the porchlight on.

Ruby's Arms

I will leave behind all of my clothes,
I wore when i was with you,
all I need's my railroad boots,
and my leather jacket,
as i say goodbye to ruby's arms,
although my heart is breaking,
i will steal away out through your
blinds, for soon you will be waking.

The morning light has washed your face,
and everything is turning blue now,
hold on to your pillow case
there's nothing i can do now,
as i say goodbye to ruby's arms,
you'll find another soldier,
and i swear to god by christmas,
there'll be someone else to hold you.

The only thing i'm taking is
the scarf off of your clothesline,
i'll hurry past your chest of drawers,
and your broken window chimes,
as i say goodbye
i'll say goodbye,
say goodbye to ruby's arms.

i'll feel my way down the darken hall,
and out into the morning,
the hobos at the freightyards,
have kept their fires burning,
so jesus christ this goddamn rain,
will someone put me on a train,

i'll never kiss your lips again,
or break your heart,
as i say goodbye
i'll say goodbye,
say goodbye to ruby's arms.

THE
EARLY
YEARS

VOLUME ONE

Goin' Down Slow

Well It's a quarter a two
and looking at you
and going down, going down slow
Well It's a quarter a two
and looking at you
and going down, going down slow

TV went off about one, we have only begun
I know that the Wednesday may come
but I have no intention of going home

Well It's a quarter a three
digging on me
and going down, going down slow

Could stay here all night,
they claim your outta sight
please get up and turn out the light
There ain't nothing better than the middle of the night

And It's a quarter a four
begging for more
and going down, going down slow
going down, going down slow
going down, going down slow
going down, going down slow

Poncho's Lament

Well the stairs sound so lonely without you
And I ain't made my bed in a week
Coffee stains on the paper I'm writing
And I'm too choked up inside to speak

And Yes, I know our differences pulled us apart
Never spoke a word heart to heart
And I'm glad that you're gone
But I wish to the lord that you'd come home
And I'm glad that you're gone
Got the feeling so strong
And I'm glad that you're gone
But I wish to the lord that you'd come home

Well my guitar still plays your favorite song
though the strings have been outta tune for some time
Every time I strum a cord, I pray out to the lord
That you'll quit your honkey-tonkin' sing my song
And I'm glad that you're gone
Got the feeling so strong
And I'm glad that you're gone
But I wish to the lord that you'd come home

So I'll throw another log onto the fire
And I'll admit I'm a lousy liar
As the coals die down and flicker
I hear that guitar picker
Play the song we used to sing so long ago
I'm glad that you're gone
Got the feeling so strong
And I'm glad that you're gone
But I wish to the lord that you'd come home

And I'm glad, damn glad you're gone
Got the feeling so strong
And I'm glad that you're gone
But I wish to the lord that you'd come home

I'm Your Late Night Evening Prostitute

Well I got here at eight and I'll be here till two
I'll try my best to entertain you and
Please don't mind me if I get a bit crude
I'm your late night evening prostitute

So drink your martinis and stare at the moon
Don't mind me I'll continue to croon
Don't mind me if I get a bit loon
I'm your late night evening prostitute

And dance, have a good time
I'll continue to shine
Yes Dance, have a good time
Don't mind me if I slip upon a rhyme

Well I got here at eight and I'll be here till two
I'll try my best to entertain you and
Please don't mind me if I get a bit crude
I'm your late night evening prostitute
I'm your late night evening prostitute

Had Me A Girl

Well I had me a girl in LA
I knew she couldn't stay
Had me a girl in San Diego
One day she just had to go
And I had me a girl Tallahassee
Boy what a foxy lassie

[chorus]

And my doctor says I'll be alright
But I'm feelin' blue
And my doctor says I'll be alright
And my doctor says I'll be alright
And my doctor says I'll be alright
But I'm feelin blue
And my doctor says I'll be alright
And my doctor says I'll be alright
And my doctor says I'll be alright

And I had me a girl in Mississippi
Oh she sure was kippy
Had me a girl in England
She done split for the mainland
And I had me a girl in New York
She up and pulled my cork

[chorus]

Then I had me a girl in North Dakota
She was just fillin' her quota
Then I had me a girl in Chula Vista

I was in love with her sister
Then I had me a girl in

[chorus]

Then I had me a girl in France
Just wanted to get in my pants
had me a girl in Toledo
Boy she sure was neato
Then I had me a girl in North Carolina
She's still on my mind

[chorus]

Rockin' Chair

Well I'm sittin' right here in my rockin chair
Running my fingers right through my hair
Fire is flicken with a yellow and gold
Makin me quiver in the snowy cold
Got a lazy old woman
Screaming bout my money
She took every cent
And she didn't leave me any

Times were never so good, got a fly for food
Got no woman to spend my money
Well she blew and took all my money

So I'm sittin' right here in my rockin chair
Running my fingers right through my hair
Spider caught the fly in his web
Do believe he may be dead

Times were never so good, got a fly for food
Got no woman to spend my money
Well she blew and took all my money

Well I'm sittin' and I'm sittin' and I'm sittin' right here
In my rockin chair
Watchin' my old dog loosing his hair

When You Ain't Got Nobody

Well when you ain't got nobody, anybody looks nice
Don't take much to make you stop and look twice
And it's either feast or famine, I've found out that it's true
And I'm hungry as a bull dog, baby how about you

And when you ain't got no big mama, all the mamas look hot
And when lovin' is you weakness, your just bound to get caught
And the story never changes, history tells it so plain
And I'll be your Dick, honey, if you'll just be my Jane

And when you ain't got nobody, anybody looks nice
It don't take much to make you stop and look twice
And it's either feast or famine, I've found out that it's true
And I'm hungry as a bull dog, baby how about you, baby how about you

Frank's Song

That woman will take you, that woman will break you
That woman will make you something you've never seen
That woman's got claws, that woman's got laws
Now look out man, you're gonna loose your mind

I had a friend, his name was Frank
He walked on the water and lord he sank
We used to go stag, now he's got a hag
It looks like Frank's got a new bag

That woman will take you, that woman will break you
That woman will make you something you've never seen
That woman's got claws, that woman's got laws
Now look out Frank, you're gonna loose your mind

What happened to Frank, can happen to you
Just find you a woman and watch what she'll do
That woman will take you, that woman's gonna break you
Look out man you're gonna loose, you're gonna loose your mind

Looks Like I'm Up Shit Creek Again

Well the sun came in my window Wednesday morning
And your love was like the golden rays again
Now I'm lying here on a Thursday, and you're lovin someone new
And it looks like I'm up shit creek again

And I can't help thinking of your lovin ways
And I cried a quart of tears since you've been gone
And I can't face the morning by myself love
And it looks like I'm up shit creek again

Since you've been gone, I cry all the time
And I cannot stand leavin you behind
So I'll pull myself together, And I'll dry away my tears
But the morning light has brought back memories
And I can't face the morning by myself love
And it looks like I'm up shit creek again

So I'm out a walkin on this dusty highway
Cause you've given me no reason for to stay
And I'll walk until I've found someone who loves me not in vain
And it looks like I'm up shit creek again
And it looks like I'm up shit creek again

So Long I'll See Ya

Mamas in the kitchen, Daddies on the phone
And nobody knows what's going on
But I've got those
so long I'll see you cause my Buick's outside waiting blues

Well one for the money, two for the show
Three to get ready, Tom's gotta go
He's got them
so long I'll see you cause my Buick's outside waiting blues

Well bye-bye-bye, well bye-bye-bye
Sing bye-bye Shooby-do-bye-bye
Gotta skeet-skat outta here, skeet-skat outta here

And mamas in the kitchen, daddies on the phone
And nobody knows what's going on
But I've got those
so long I'll see you cause my Buick's outside waiting blues

Well Tommy's gotta skeet-skat, skeet-skat outta here
Skeet-skat right outta here
And one for the money, two for the show
Three to get ready, I gotta go
'Cause I've got them
so long I'll see you cause my Buick's outside waiting blues
And skeet-skat outta here, gonna skeet-skat outta here,
Gonna skeet-skatJoutta here, gonna skeet-skat outta here
Got so long I'll see you cause my Buick's outside waiting blues
Gonna skeet-skat outta here, gonna skeet-skat outta here,
Gonna skeet-skatJoutta here, gonna skeet-skat outta here
I got solongI'llseeyoucausemyBuick'soutsidewaitingblues

THE
EARLY
YEARS

VOLUME TWO

Mockin' Bird

Mocking Bird high in a tree
Looks like you got the best of me
Mocking Bird singing his song
Well Mocking Bird mocking me
now that you're gone

Mocking Bird high in a loof
Well he's blowing notes on top my roof
Mocking Bird singing his song
Well Mocking Bird mocking me
now that you're gone.

Mocking Bird high in a tree
Looking up at you, you're looking down at me
Mocking Bird high in a loof
Well he's blowing notes on top my roof.

Mocking Bird high in a tree
Looking up at you, you're looking down at me
Mocking Bird singing his song
Well Mocking Bird mocking me
now that you're gone.

Throwed some papers, tried to scare him away
Just looked down at me and this is what he said

Mocking Bird high in a tree
Looks like you got the best of me
Mocking Bird singing his song
Well Mocking Bird mocking me
now that you're gone

In Between Love

In between love and trying to scheme love
Who can tell what we may find
Never thought love, not get caught love
Between the magic in your eyes
And loves like women, it's cool and breezy
Never thought that love could be so easy

In between love and trying to scheme love
And in between love again
In between love and trying to scheme love
Who can tell what we may find
All this time love, I sublime love
To the feelings in my mind
Loves like women, it's cool and breezy
Never thought that love could be so easy

In between love and trying to scheme love
And in between love again

Blue Skies

Blue skies over my head
Give me another reason to get out of bed
And blue skies shine on my face
Give me another woman to take her place

Ain't got no money, cupboards are bare
No cigarettes and the kids got nothing to wear
She walked out without a word
Now the only sound left is the morning bird
singing . . .

Blue skies over my head
Give me another reason to get out of bed
And blue skies shine on my face
Give me another woman to take her place

Blue skies over my head
Give me another reason to get out of bed
And blue skies shine on my face
Give me another woman to take her place
Give me another woman to take her place

I Want You

I want you, you, you
All I want is you, you, you
All I want is you

Give you the stars above, Sun on the brightest day
Give you all my love, if you would only say
I want you, you, you
All I want is you, you, you
All I want is you

So It Goes

If I was a seagull high and aloof
I'd sail to the highest perch on your roof
But I ain't no seagull, you know my name
And the wind's blowin fortune, the wind's blowin pain
And so it goes, nobody knows
How to get to the sky, how to get to the sky

If I was a puppy dog in the early dawn
I'd make it to your house and sleep on your lawn
but I ain'ty no puppydog, you know my name
And the wind blows fortune, the wind blows pain
And so it goes, nobody knows
How to get to the sky, how to get to the sky
How to get to the sky, how to get to the sky

ONE FROM THE HEART

Is There Any Way Out Of This Dream?

I can clearly see nothing as clear
I keep falling apart every year
Let's take a hammer to it
There's no glamour in it
Is there any way out of this dream?

I'm as blue as I can possibly be
Is there someone else out there for me
Summer is dragging its feet
I feel so incomplete
Is there any way out of this dream?

Summer is dragging its feet
I feel so incomplete
Is there any way out of this dream?

Picking Up After You

Here comes the bride, and there goes the groom
Looks like a hurricane went through this room
Smells like a pool hall, where's my other shoe
And I'm sick and tired of pickin' up after you

Looks like you spent the night in a trench
And tell me, how long have you been combin' your hair with a wrench
The roses are dead and the violets are too
And I'm sick and tired of pickin' up after you

Well, I've told you before, I won't tell you again
You don't defrost the icebox with a ball point pen
This railroad apartment is held together with glue
And I'm sick and tired of pickin' up after you

Because I know I've been swindled, ı never bargained for this
What's more, you never cared about me
Why don't you get your own place so you can live like you do
And I'm sick and tired of pickin' up after you

Take all your relatives and all of your shoes
Believe me, I'II really swing when you're gone
I'II be living on chicken and wine after we're through
With someone I pick up after you
With someone I pick up after you
With someone I pick up after you
With someone I pick up after you

Old Boyfriends

Old boyfriends
Lost in the pocket of your overcoat
Like burned out light bulbs on a Ferris Wheel
Old boyfriends

You remember the kinds of cars they drove
Parking in an orange grove
He fell in love, you see
With someone that I used to be

Though I very seldom think of him
Nevertheless sometimes a mannequin's
Blue summer dress can make the window like a dream
Ah, but now those dreams belong to someone else
Now they talk in their sleep
In a drawer where I keep all my

Old boyfriends
Remember when you were burning for them
Why do you keep turning them into
Old boyfriends

They look you up when they're in town
To see if they can still burn you down
He fell in love, you see
With someone that I used to be

Though I very seldom think of him
Nevertheless sometimes a mannequin's
Blue summer dress can make the window like a dream
Ah, but now those dreams belong to someone else

Now they talk in their sleep
In a drawer where I keep all my

Old boyfriends
Turn up every time it rains
Fall out of the pages in a magazine
Old boyfriends

Girls fill up the bars every spring
Not places for remembering
Old boyfriends
All my old boyfriends
Old boyfriends

Broken Bicycles

Broken bicycles, old busted chains
With rusted handle bars, out in the rain
Somebody must have an orphanage for
All these things that nobody wants any more

September's reminding July
It's time to be saying goodbye
Summer is gone, but our love will remain
Like old broken bicycles out in the rain

Broken bicycles, don't tell my folks
There's all those playing cards pinned to the spokes
Laid down like skeletons out on the lawn
The wheels won't turn when the other has gone

The seasons can turn on a dime
Somehow I forget every time
For all the things that you've given me will always stay
Broken, but I'll never throw them away

I Beg Your Pardon

I'm just a scarecrow without you
Baby, please don't disappear
I beg your pardon, dear

I got a bottle for a trumpet
And a hatbox for a drum
And I beg your pardon, dear

I got upset, I lost my head
I didn't mean the things I said
You are the landscape of my dreams
Darling, I beg your pardon

I'd give you Boardwalk and Park Place
And all of my hotels
I beg your pardon, dear

Please don't go back to St. Louis
Can't you tell that I'm sincere
I beg your pardon, dear

I got upset, I lost my head
I didn't mean the things I said
You are the landscape of my dreams
Darling, I beg your pardon

Little Boy Blue

Little Boy Blue, come blow your horn
The dish ran away with the spoon
Home again, home again Saturday morn
He never gets up before noon

Well, she used to render you legal and tender
When you used to send her your promises, boy
A diller, a dollar, unbutton your collar
And come out and holler out all of your noise

So Little Boy Blue, come blow your top
And cut it right dawn to the quick
Don't sit home and cry on the Fourth of July
Around now you're hittin' the bricks

So abracadabra, now she disappeared
Everything's Canada Dry
So watch your behavior and rattle your cage
With a bottle of Bourbon, goodbye

So Little Boy Blue lost little Bo Peep
She fell through a hole in the nest
Now ain't it peculiar that she's finally cooled

Your big wheel's just like all of the rest

Whenever it rains, the umbrellas complain
They always get played for a chump

So mark it and strike it, she's history now
And you're hangin' out at the pump

Little Boy Blue, come blow your horn
The dish ran away with the spoon
Home again, home again Saturday morn
He never gets up before noon

Well, she used to render you legal and tender
When you used to send her your promises boy
A diller, a dollar, unbutton your collar
And come out and holler out all of your noise

You Can't Unring A Bell

You can't unring a bell, Junior
It'll cost you to get out of this one, Junior
She's got big plans that don't include you
Take it like a man

Cause you, you can't unring a bell, sucker
You'll need an attorney for this journey, Junior

How's it feel
How do you like it in the slam
You're a little man in a great big town
Perhaps you were a little hasty
He-he-he-he-he-he-he
You can't take back the things you said, man

Cause you can't unring a bell, Junior
Ah, hurts don't it
Take it like a man
Get it through your head
Suffer
He-he-he-he-he-he-he

This One's From The Heart

I should go out and honk the horn, it's Independence Day
But instead I just pour myself a drink
It's got to be love, I've never felt this way
Oh baby, this one's from the heart

The shadows on the wall look like a railroad track
I wonder if he's ever comin' back
The moon's a yellow stain across the sky
Oh baby, this one's from the heart

Maybe I'll go down to the corner and get a racin' form
But I should prob'ly wait here by the phone
And the brakes need adjustment on the convertible
Oh baby, this one's from the heart

The worm is climbin' the avocado tree
Rubbin' its back against the wall
I pour myself a double sympathy
Oh baby, this one's from the heart

Blondes, brunettes, and redheads put their hammer down
To pound a cold chisel through my heart.
But they were nothin' but apostrophes
Oh baby, this one's from the heart

I can't tell, is that a siren or a saxophone?
But the roads get so slippery when it rains
I love you more than all these words can ever say
Oh baby, this one's from the heart

Take Me Home

Take me home, you silly boy
Put your arms around me
Take me home, you silly boy
All the world's not round without you

I'm so sorry that I broke your heart
Please don't leave my side
Take me home, you silly boy
Cause I'm still in love with you

Once Upon a Town

I wish I had a dollar
for each time I took a chance
On all those two-bit Romeos
who counterfeit romance

Somehow always thinking
of the last time I fell down
Knowing that you fall in love
once upon a town

The Wages of Love

Down through the ages, all of the sages
Said, "don't spend your wages on love"
There's graft and collusion about the intrusion
And preceding foreclosures, there's overexposure

Down at the crossroads the question is posed
The bridge is washed out and the highway is closed
Got every reason to firmly believe
Love was designed to exploit and deceive

There's an attendant, wherever you send 'em
that red ball and descend your chest, you will see
Simple addition keeps with tradition
Don't spend your wages on love

Take any burgh, any city or town
Just get on main street and drive all the way down
You see, love has a graveyard nurtured for those
That fell on their sabers and paid through the nose

Your shovel's a shot glass, dig your own hole
Bury what's left of your miserable soul
Down thru the ages, all of the sages
Said don't spend your wages on love